POLITICAL THEORY - I

PAPER : C-1 (FOR B.A. 1ST SEMESTER STUDENTS OF BODOLAND UNIVERSITY)

RITURAJ BASUMATARY

Made with ♥ on the Notion Press Platform
www.notionpress.com

Contents

CHAPTER I

Introducing Political Theory

Political Theory is one of the core areas in political science. It is only in recent times that it has emeged as an academic discipline. Earlier, those who engaged in this enterprise styled themselves as philosophers or scientiests. From ancient Greece to the present, the history of political theory has dealt with fundamental and perennial ideas of political science. The first modern usage of the term political science was in the works of Montesquieu, Adam Smith, Adam Ferguson & David Hume, where it meant the science of the legislator.

Political Theory is the most appropriate term to employ in designating that intellectual tradition which affirms the possibility of transcending the sphere of immediately practical concerns and viewing man's societal existence from critical perspective. Political Theory was political science in the full sense and there could be no science without theoretical.

Definition of political theory

According to David Held - Political Theory is a network of concepts and generalisations about political life involving ideas, assumptions and statements about the nature, purpose and key features of government, state and society and about the political capabilities of human beings.

WC Coker explained that "When political government and it's forms and activities are studied not simply as facts to be described and compared and judged in reference to their immediate temporary effects, but as to be understood and appraised in relation to the constant needs, desires and opinion of men, then we have political theory.

Andrew Hacker described that political theory is a combination of disinterested search for the principles of good state and good society on the other hand and a disinterested search for knowledge of political and social reality on the other hand.

Norman Barry defined that political theory is an electric subject draws upon a variety of discipline. There is no body of knowledge or method of analysis which can be classified as belonging exclusively to political theory.

Political Theory and Political Thought

It is generally believed that political thought is the general thought comprising of theories and values of all those persons or a section of the community who think and write day to day activities, policies and decisions of the state and which has a bearing on our present living. These persons can be writers, philosophers, journalists, poets, political commentators etc. Political Thought has a fixed form and can be in the form of treatise, speeches, political commentaries etc. What is important about political thought is that it is time bound since the policies and programs of the governments change from time to time.

On the other hand, Political Theory provides a model of explanation of political reality as it is understood by the writer. As such there can be many different political theory of the same period. Also political theory is based on certain discipline - be it philosophy, history, economics or sociology. And lastly since the task of theory is not only to explain the political reality but also to change it (or to resist change), political theory can be conservative, critical or revolutionary. According to Barker, while political thought is the immanent of a whole age, political theory is the speculation of a particular thinker. While political thought is implicit and immersed in the stream of vital action, political theory is explicit and may be detached from the political reality of a particular period.

Political Theory and Political Philosophy

Philosophy is called science of wisdom. Wisdom about this world, man or God. When this wisdom is applied into the study of political phenomena or the state, it is called political philosophy. It belongs to the category of normative political theory. It is concerned with not only explaining what is but also what ought to be. Political Philosophy is not concerned with contemporary issues but with certain universal issues in the political life of man such as nature and purpose of political organization, basis of political authority, nature of rights, liberty, equality, justice etc.

The distinction between political philosophy and political theory is explained by the fact that whereas a political philosopher is a political theorist, but a political theorist may not necessary be a political philosopher. For example, David Easton is an eminent political theorist but is not considered a political philosopher. In other words while political philosophy is abstract or speculative, political theory can be both normative and empirical.

Political Theory is concerned both with political institutions and the ideas and aspirations that form the basis of those institutions. However, we must not forget that though we can analytically distinguish between philosophy and theory, yet political theory is separated from political philosophy, it's meaning will appear distorted and it will prove barren and irrelevant. We can say that political theory must be supplemented by philosophy.

Political Theory and Political Science

As a discipline, political science is much more comprehensive and includes a different forms of speculation in politics such as political thought, political theory, political philosophy, political ideology, institutional or structural framework, comparative politics, public administration, international law & organization etc. With the rise of political science as a separate discipline, political theory was made one of its subfields. However political science refers to the study of politics by the use of scientific methods in contrast to political philosophy, which is free to follow intuition.

Political Science is concerned with describing and explaining the realities of political behaviour, generalisations about man and political institutions on empirical evidence and the role of power in society. Political Theory on the other hand is not only concerned about the behavioural study of the political phenomena from empirical point of view but also prescribing the goals which states, governments, societies and citizens ought to pursue. Political Theory also aims to generalize about the right conduct in the political life and about the legitimate use of power.

Characteristics of political theory

We can identify the following characteristics of political theory

1. Political theory is theory of politics. It seeks to understand, analysis and explain the phenomena of politics. If also attempts to reform by rectifying the shortcomings in political life of society.

2. Political theory like an ideology also includes a set of beliefs, values and ideas which stand accepted by the people in the process of their governance.

3. Political theory involves systematic reflections on politics or state or government or political institutions.

4. Political theory can be normative or empirical or both. Description, analysis, explanation, prediction and change are the goals of political theory.

6. Scope of political theory covers all areas of political relations. Finally political theory is related to the state, government and political institutions.

Decline of political theory

According to David Easton

1. Historicism - According to David Easton, writers such as Dunning, Sabine, Mcliwain, Lindsay, Carlye are more interested in describing the causes for rise of an ideology, system of values etc. They do not engage in stimulating their own thought to find solutions to contemporary social problems.

2. Moral relativism - Easton accuses Hume & Weber of having relativistic attitude towards "values" and neglecting what consequences do they have for the facts. However a political scientist to be sensitive towards social problems, contrast values and not transplant them.

3. Confusing science and theory - Easton accuses the political theorist of using science and theory in a wrong way. In fact he points out that mere use of scientific method can not generate theories. The latter task involves identifying major variable and establishing a harmonious relationship between them.

4. Hyper factualism - Easton accuses writers like Paul Bryce of using theory simply to accumulate facts. Such tendencies in his opinion fail to relate themselves with the significant problems in a political system.

According to Cobban, he presents a very pessimistic picture of political theory. He holds that despite being an intellectually rich tradition since the time of Plato, there has been a death of such work since 18th century. Among the external causes for the decline of political theory, he mentions increasing role of the state and bureaucratic machinery and military establishment.

According to Germino - Despite being an advocate of decline thesis, he is optimistic about it's future. Like Cobban, he locates the decline of political theory to the growing ascendency of scientism. But he also brings in what he describes as ideological reductionism found in the works of Tracy, Comte and Marx.

Resurgence of political theory

Resurgence is multifaceted pluralism. The main resurgence was found in USA where American Political Science Association and Rockefeller Foundation played the pioneer role. A large number of scholars gathered at various Research Institutes and Universities of America and their painstaking efforts really enriched the empirical approach to the study of political theory leading to its resurgence.

The resurgence in political theory that took place after the second world war assumed various shapes and manifestation. One such manifestation is pluralism. Pluralism wants to emphasis that in any society there are numerous individuals who cherish different tastes, interests and values. It has a clear liberal lineage.

Even during the day of traditional political theory there existed pluralism. After the second world war political theory received larger impetus from many sources. Varieties of ideas and concepts rapidly developed due to the advance of pluralism and this help the resurgence of political theory.

Behaviouralism

Behaviouralism constitute a very important aspects of the resurgence of political theory that took place at the beginning of the fifties of the last century. After a thorough analysis of the behaviour, facts and datas, certain conclusions and models of political theory can be constructed. Behaviouralism in political science also states that it does not deal with all sorts of behaviour of individuals but only with that behaviour which displays political character.

Rawls' normative theory

Rawls says justice is the first virtue of social institutions as truth is the system of thought. In the opinion of Rawls any social theory, all organizations and institutions must aim at ensuring justice and if the authority is fails to do this the entire social structure will faced crisis and numerous problems.

According to Rawls both moral theory and natural science must begin with data. The data for science are empirical observation and the data for ethical theory are moral judgments. In this way Rawls tried to prove that moral theory can not be aside or ignored on the ground that it is not based on empiricism. Rawls' attempt is really revolutionary and it poses a great challenge to Easton behaviouralism.

Major schools of political theory

Political Science has been both a very old as well as a new discipline. In contemporary times a synthetic approach (Empirical normative or scientific-classical approach i.e. an integrated approach) is being followed for studying and theorising all aspects of politics comprehensively, realistically and precisely.

Let us study five major streams of political theory.

1. Classical political theory-

Classical political theory emerged in ancient Greek. The exercise began with Plato and Aristotle and continued up to the 19th century. It remained engaged in search for a perfect and ideal state. It included politics, the idea of theory and the practice of philosophy.

Politics referred to participation in the public affairs, theory referred to the systematic knowledge gained through observation and philosophy referred to the quest for reliable knowledge. Thus political theory was a systematic inquiry to acquire reliable knowledge about matters concerning public affairs.

2. Liberal political theory-

In the 18th & 19th centuries democratization of political process took place in several European states. The increase in the size of a modern democratic nation state and the progress of industrial revolution created an environment which produce a big change in the nature of political theory. The classical political theory began giving a place to liberal theory of politics with its main focus on such issues as rights, liberty, equality, property, justice, functions of state etc. We can say that the central theme of liberal political theory was individualism.

3. Marxist political theory-

Marxist political theory is a theory of social change and revolutionary reconstitution of society. Liberal political theory was rejected by Karl Marx, Engels and their followers Lenin, Stalin and others. They formulated, adopted and used Marxian political theory which project itself as a theory of scientific socialism. It had for its basis several fundamental theories - dialectical, historical materialism, economic determinism, class struggle and surplus value. It rejected capitalism as an evil system and projected the state as the tool, an organised power of the capitalists for exploiting and ruling the poor. Marxian political theory strongly criticised and rejected the liberal theory which was projected as the ideology of capitalism.

4. Empirical-scientific political theory

In the 20th century, particularly after the end of second world war, a revolt developed against the classical tradition of normative political theory when several political scientist (the Behavioualist) got involved in building a scientific-empirical theory of politics. In the early 20th century Max Weber, Graham Wallas and Bentley gave an empirical dimension to the study of political theory and advocated that its study should be based upon facts only. The behaviouralist advocated the need for building a true science of political through use of empirical scientific methods. They rejected the studies of values and advocated concentration on facts of politics.

5. Contemporary political theory-

Since 1970s, there has been a revival of interest in political theory in USA, Europe and other parts of the world. Whether it is Marxism or Socialism, liberalism or democracy - all stand challenged and new powerful social movements are seeking to redraw the issues in political theory. During the era of domination of behaviouralism, political theory was overpowered by political science. In its contemporary form both empirical and normative studies are being conducted. It now definitely reflects a new interest in normative political theory. A number of political issues and problems like human rights, environment, ecology, feminism, sustainable development, globalization and others are being systematically described as well analysed.

Significance of political theory

Political Theory can help the society to reform it's institutions and relations by adopting values and concept in social, political and economic processes and relations.

Political Theory can play an important role in the development of political science as a social discipline. Political Theory is a tool of political science and is a valuable sub field of political science. Relationship between the individual and the state. It offers a vision of ideal political institutions and can guide the process of political. It also offers empirical explanations of various processes and dimensions of politics.

Conclusion

Political Theory is one of the core areas in political science. It is only in recent times that it has emerged as an academic discipline. Earlier, those who engaged in this enterprise styled themselves as philosopher or scientists. From ancient Greece to the present, the history of political theory has dealt with fundamental and perennial ideas of political science. The first modern usage of the term political science was in the works of Charles-louis de secondat Montesquieu (1689-1755), Adam Smith (1723-90), Adam Ferguson (1723-1816) and David Hume (1711-76) where it meant the science of the legislature.

Political Theory is the most appropriate term to employ in designating that intellectual tradition which affirms the possibility of transcending the sphere of immediate practical concerns and viewing man societed existence from a critical perspectives. Political Theory was a political science in the full sense and there could be no science without theory.

CHAPTER II

What is Politics: Theorizing the 'Political'

Aristotle, the father of Political Science, first made use of the term 'Politics' for his treatise on the state. The term 'Politics' is derived from the Latin word 'Politicus' which in turn is derived from the Greek word 'Polis'. In Greek 'Polis' means city state and the subject that studies its activities is Politics.

The Greeks were the first to conduct a systematic study of Political Science. The Sophists were the first expounders of Political Theory. Later on, Socrates, Plato and Aristotle conducted scientific investigation into the various problems of the state.

The Greeks lived in City States and they made no distinction between a city and a state. We live in large territorial states today, but the Greek meaning can be extended to the study of the modern state also. 'Politics' today is known by the new nomenclature of 'Political Science'. The term 'Political Science' (Science Politique) was coined by the French writer Jean Bodin in the sixteenth century. Political Science is a Social Science systematically dealing with the various problems of the State and the Government.

In other words, Politics generally means struggle for power. Whatever may be the ultimate aim of Politics, but its immediate aim is always power. For example Indian National Congress (INC) vs. Bharatiya Janata Party (BJP) are the example of National Politics in our country.

Political Theory: Meaning and Definition

Before analyzing the definitions of Political Theory as given by some Political Scientists, let us understand the meaning of the two words: 'Political' and 'Theory'.

A. Political

The word 'Political' is the adjective of 'Politics'. In a traditional sense, it means relating to polis i.e. state and government. However in contemporary times, the term 'Political' is defined in a broader way. It means power and power relations. Political relations involve power to a significant extent. Lasswell and Kaplan define Politics as the study of "the shaping and sharing of power".

B. Theory

Theory can be defined as a set of interrelated propositions/principles/concepts which are designed to explain and synthesise the ideas and conclusions or generalizations pertaining to a discipline. In its traditional form, theory is a normative exercise. It explains and prescribes values and offers a philosophy of the concerned subject. In its modern form, theory is taken to mean a set of tested and valid generalizations arrived at through the use of scientific method of study. It is conceptualized as scientific theory. Several modern scholars however, accept both these forms of theory i.e. normative theory and empirical scientific theory.

Definitions of Political Theory

"Political Theory includes political science and political philosophy". – George Catlin

"A combination of disinterested search for the principles of good state and good society on the one hand and a search for knowledge of political and social reality on the other". – Andrew Hacker

"In a very broad sense political theory is anything about politics or relevant to politics. However, in its specific and narrow sense, it is the disciplined investigation of political problems."

Features/Nature/Characteristics of Political Theory

We can identify the following features or nature or characteristics of Political Theory:-

(a) Political Theory is Theory of Politics which seeks to understand, analyse and explain the phenomena of politics.

(b) Political Theory attempts to reform by rectifying the shortcomings in the political life of society.

(c) Political Theory, like an ideology also includes a set of beliefs, values and ideas, which stand accepted by the people in the process of their governance.

(d) Political Theory involves a systematic reflections on politics or state or government or political institutions.

(e) Political Theory is generally the intellectual and moral creation of a single thinker who offers a theoretical explanation of the political reality – the phenomena of state.

(f) Political Theory can be normative or empirical or both.

(e) Description, analysis, explanation, prediction and change are the goals of Political Theory.

(f) Scope of Political Theory covers all areas of political relations.

(g) Political Theory is the handiwork of philosophers, historian, economists, theologians, sociologist, thinkers, journalists, intellectuals and all others who try to comprehend and explain the political reality.

(h) Finally, Political Theory is related to the state, government and political institutions.

Scope of Political Theory

Political Theory stands for history of political ideas. The earlier political thinkers devoted mainly on the point of distinction between 'state' and 'government'. They regarded 'state' as a collectivity for the sake of promoting some common purpose and 'government' as its instrument for implementing the will of the community. Till the first half of the 19th century, Political Theory was concerned with the study of 'state' and 'government'. Political Theory as understood in modern times devotes to the study of power. It deals with all those activities connected with the 'struggle for power'.

The modern political scientists point out distinction between 'government' and 'politics'. The basic area of the earlier thinker's concern were the institutional frameworks of the rule of the states like the structure and procedure of the legislative and executive bodies, local self government, political parties, voting etc. which are responsible for the conduct of government.

Political Theory is therefore not only concerned with the study of 'state' and 'government' as conceived till the mid 20th century; it is also presently understood as the study of 'power'. It covers all those activities that are connected with 'power' and the 'struggle for power'.

Importance of Political Theory

Political Theory is useful for us as it helps in understanding the meaning of political concepts by looking at the way they are understood and used in ordinary language.

Political theories debate and examine the various meanings and opinions from different contexts in a systematic manner.

The four ways in which the political theory can be useful to us are:

It helps in understanding how constitutions are shaped in a certain manner, how governments and social lives are arranged in a certain systematic manner by studying and understanding the ideas and principles that are at their base.

It shows the significance of various principles such as rule of law, separation of power, judicial review etc.

Political theory helps bureaucrats, politicians, government officers and advocates to interpret the laws and constitution. It also helps in understanding the problems of society and explore the ways to solve them.

Political theory encourages individuals to examine their ideas and feelings about political things so that they can become moderate in their ideas and feelings.

Different Views of Politics

Marxism

Marxism refers to the political and economic theories brought out by Karl Marx, especially with regard to the capitalistic social structure. Marx analyzed the social structure based on the economic activities and according to him, economy is one of the main requirements for humans to satisfy their needs. There are economic organizations that have been formed in such a way that they decide the social relations, ideologies, political and legal systems between social classes. The forces of production may have unequal relationships and profit sharing, which will lead them to the class struggle. The result of the class struggle will be the Socialism, which is said to have a cooperative ownership in production. However, later on, this Socialism will pave the way to Communism that is the ideal social structure in Marx's point of view and there will neither be social classes nor states but the common ownership of the means of production. This is the simplest idea of Marxism and this theory has been applied in so many other subjects as well. However, it is said that there is no single definitive theory of Marxism.

Liberalism

Liberalism can be identified as a political philosophy that emphasizes the idea of being free and liberate. This idea of being free could be applied to many concepts and situations, but liberalists focus more on democracy, civil rights, property ownership, religion, etc. in general. It was during the period of Enlightenment that this philosophy of Liberalism came into the field. The philosopher called John Locke is said to have introduced this concept. Liberalists rejected the absolute monarchy, the state religion and the immense power and authority of kings etc. Instead of the monarchy, liberalists promoted democracy. However, Liberalism gained much attention after the French Revolution and today it is a powerful influencing political force throughout the world.

Marxism vs Liberalism

The difference between Marxism and Liberalism stems from the key idea around which each of these concepts are built. Both Marxism and Liberalism are concepts that are espoused by people all over the world. Marxism was introduced by Karl Marx to explain the changes and developments in the society as a result of the conflict between the elites and the working class people. Liberalism, on the other hand, emphasizes the idea of being free and equal with regard to certain concepts like religion, trade, political freedom, civil rights, etc. Marxism focuses more on establishing a classless society that is called the "Communism" and Liberalism is just a movement that stresses the freedom in behavior or attitudes of individuals. Let us look at these two ideologies: namely Marxism and Liberalism and the difference between them in detail.

When we look at both these concepts, we can identify some similarities. Both have relationships with economic, political and social aspects of a particular society. Both deal with the state of human beings living in the society.

- When we look at differences, we can see that Marxism is a theory whereas Liberalism is an ideology.
- Marxism talks of a social transition and in contrast Liberalism deals with the individual state of being.

However, both theses are very popular in the modern world and they are upheld by many communities around the world.

Communitarian View

According to the communitarian view, the essence of human nature lies in the spirit of cooperation, not conflict. Hence mutual aid and cooperation is the foundation of political organisation. Communitarian sees no basic conflict between the interests of different members of society.

Historical Development of Political Theory

Classical Political Theory:

What we call political theory today is not the product of any particular period or the by-product of research of any single person or few persons. Rather there is a history of development behind which lies the work and research as well as philosophy of numerous persons.

Political scientists and researchers have felt that the political theory can be divided into few stages and some of these are classical political theory, traditional political theory, modern political theory and post-modern political theory. It is to be noted here that this classification is not final. Many political scientists do not agree with this classification. But for clarity of thought and convenience of analysis this classification may be followed.

One aspect of classical political theory is it was dominated by certain eternal values and philosophy. This is specifically to be found in the writings of Plato, Aristotle and some others. Both the Greek philosophers thought of establishing ideal state though the modus operandi of both of them was not same.

But there is a resemblance between the ideal states of Plato and Aristotle. To Plato the mechanism of setting up an ideal state was to entrust a philosopher king with the task of administration of the ideal state because it was believed that he would be able to keep himself above narrow interests and ensure communism of wife, children and property.

Plato believed that in an ideal state there shall be uniformity in education, mode of living etc. But his disciple Aristotle did not give any importance to uniformity. He relied upon the abolition of different forms of inequalities and he arrived at the conclusion that only in polity there can exist such an arrangement.

Both Plato and Aristotle were enamoured by the concepts of good and noble life and they thought that eternal values, goodness and nobleness of life can be realised only through the state and for that reason they were thinking of an ideal state.

Only through unconditional surrender to the authority of ideal state an individual can build up his goodness and nobleness of character. Thus, in the thought system of Plato and Aristotle ethics, philosophy, morality, eternal values etc. were completely mixed together.

In the writings of Plato and Aristotle and many others rationality had a very crucial role to play. Since men are rational they are not supposed to disobey the diktat of eternal values, morality and idealism. Throughout the middle Ages there was a long standing and damaging conflict between the church and the state and the central theme of this conflict was state and politics should be controlled by church and religion.

Some medieval thinkers such as St. Augustine (354-430), St. Thomas Aquinas (1227- 1274) and Marsilius of Padua (1270-1340) were all religious-minded and honest persons. All of them thought of state and politics in the light of religion and honesty. So the classical political theory was shrouded with morality, ethics, religious conceptions and many subjective notions.

Natural Law and Classical Political Theory:

Not only morality, ethics and eternal values managed a vintage position in the classical political theory, concept of natural law earned abundant prominence, wide publicity and approval of large number of philosophers in this stage of political theory. We have already noted that both Plato and Aristotle were profusely influenced by rationalism. Natural law had also a great impact upon their political thought and general ideas.

A large number of thinkers believed that the natural law was the greatest manifestation of reason, rationality, correctness and human intellect. Rational knowledge, goodness, reasonability, justice, structured reality and morality are all embedded in natural law. Politicians, statesmen, philosophers and even a large number of educated people were inclined to give maximum importance to natural law.

In the whole period of classical political theory people were reluctant to give any credence to man-made laws, natural law was the real guiding force of all activities and particularly the political activities of state and men.

The exponents of the classical political theory were so much imbued with the thought and importance of natural law that they started to think both natural law and rationalism as the two sides of the same coin and here the coin is society and its political structure.

The influence of natural law was so much prominent in earlier periods that Christian thinkers and philosophers could not come out of its influence. We know that both Hobbes and Locke paid a good deal of attention to the concept of natural law. They wanted to build up a civil society through the instrumentality of contract.

But even the society made by contract could not get rid of the overwhelming influence of natural law. Many thinkers wanted to build up future society upon the natural law and in their thought and attempt utopianism played the most vital role. They thought of a golden age and good society the basis of which would be natural law. In Rousseau's political thought we find a very fine combination of Plato's idealism, morality and natural law.

Rousseau thought that only the revival of state of nature and that is through the system of contract an ideal society could be built up. Even Marx was not free from the influence of natural law. He tells us that in ancient society there was no discrimination among men and also no exploitation. Everything was managed by law of nature.

The emergence of private property which is an innovation of some men heavily told upon the efficacy of natural law. Natural law was replaced by man made laws and this precipitated the exploitation and degradation of society. Hence we see that classical political theory was dominated by idealism, ethics and natural law.

Modern Traditional Political Theory:

It is very difficult to say assertively when the appearance of modern political theory actually took place and subsequently to thrive but there is an almost agreement in this regard that after Machiavelli (1469-1527) the political theory began to assume a different shape because of the fact that he was the first thinker who strongly advocated for forging a separation between politics and religion.

This attempt of Machiavelli initiated a new trend in political theory and it is politics or political theory has a separate existence and both must maintain separate identity. Machiavelli performed a good job by assertively advocating the divorce between religion and politics. But in spite of this after Machiavelli political theory could not assert itself. Religion clandestinely and sometimes overtly began to influence political theory.

He was thus a political thinker of transition period. West European society was not completely free from the influence of religion. In the political thought of Christian thinkers religion had an important part to play. That is why post-Machiavellian political theory was both modern and traditional.

Modern in the sense that the tremendous influence of church and religion on politics and functions of state that existed in the Middle Ages began to recede. But religion was still a force to reckon with. Hence post-classical political theory is sometimes called modern traditional political theory.

The State as a Machine:

The important characteristic feature of political theory of the modern traditional period is that the state is a machine. In the classical period the state was also considered as a vehicle through which men can realise their noble aspirations. But this role of state could not earn widespread approval from wider sections of society because people were not profoundly interested in ethical, moral and ideological values.

The two exponents of contract theory—Hobbes and Locke—introduced a new thought and vision and it is that the state is a machine through which individuals can achieve certain ends which are associated with their ground to earth life and existence.

According to Hobbes these are peace and security and according to Locke the chief objectives of any political organisation (Locke also uses the term civil society) to ascertain life and liberty and to make proper arrangements for the protection of private property. The political theory adumbrated by Locke unfolded a new concept and it is liberalism. Liberalism is a very complex concept that embraces so many ideas and views and in fact modern traditional theory revolves around this particular concept.

On the other hand, Hobbes gave very little attention to the protection of property and realisation of liberty. To him security and peace were of utmost importance. However, during the early years of modern political theory state appeared to be a machine and the machine was considered to be powerful. To sum up, in the modern traditional period the state has primarily been viewed as a machine and the inner meaning is that the state has been set up to fulfill certain limited functions just like machine. A particular machine is manufactured to do a particular job.

Individualism and Democracy:

Individualism and democracy received tremendous encouragement and support from the writings of a number of thinkers many of whom were well known. In the political thought of Hobbes and Locke individualism was greatly emphasized. Both the contract thinkers considered various rights as of prime importance. Though Hobbes was a great monarchist and not a democrat in our sense, he treated people's right to take food and medicine very important.

Hobbes also said that no authority had any power to force man form taking food and medicine. Priority was always given to man and his all round development and it was firmly believed that if the importance of state is not brought to minimum level individual's freedom could never be achieved and mainly for that reason in Western democracy man was always given utmost importance.

In this period theory of natural rights was treated with special care. It was believed that since the state was not the creator of rights it cannot take them away from individuals. It was also strongly argued that individual and his rights existed before the establishment of civil society and government and because of this the rights of man must always get first importance. In this way in the stage of modern political theory individual was deliberately brought into the limelight. The best way to protect the rights of individuals is to bind both with contract.

The political thinkers of modern traditional period also focused their attention on individualism because they thought that non-interference on the activities of man was the best for man's progress. It was thought that only democracy was a viable form of government and through it people can develop their inherent qualities.

It is said that though Hobbes was a worshipper of absolutism it cannot be assertively said that he hated democracy. Locke, Rousseau and a score of thinkers were staunch believers of democracy though the forms they advocated were not uniform types. In this connection we can remember Jefferson's famous dictum that government governs best that governs least. Today what we call minimal state in the early modern period that concept was advocated by many celebrities and Jefferson was one of them.

Emancipation of individual became practically the core idea of many political philosophers. Wasby writes "Modern democracy the rise of Protestantism and the development of capitalism are all associated with the emancipation of the individual in Western political thought". Hence democracy and individualism in this period developed simultaneously. But these two concepts were not the solitary occupiers of the entire thought system of this period. Democracy was viewed from different standpoints.

Capitalism and Marxism:

Two important tributaries of political theory that earned prominence in the modern period are capitalism and Marxism. Several states of Western Europe witnessed unprecedented changes in social, political and economic fields in the second half of the eighteenth century and those changes were considered the tangible products of Industrial Revolution.

Industrial Revolution generated fabulous amount of wealth and goods but a major part of which went to a microscopic fraction of society who used it for its own consumption and for further generation of wealth. Through this from the very beginning of nineteenth century developed a new phenomenon which is popularly known as capitalism. The most unpopular product of capitalism is the inequality of income and wealth.

This inequality of wealth and income created a lot of resentment among a large number of thinkers and Karl Marx tops the list. He squarely blamed capitalism for the growing misery of working class. He also believed that the bourgeois state machinery was manipulated by the capitalists in their favour.

Marx's sweeping conclusion was that only a protracted class struggle and permanent revolution can emancipate the common people from the exploitation of capitalist class. From Marxism there arose another doctrine which constituted a very important aspect of modern political theory and it is socialism. Some of its forms are Scientific Socialism, Fabian Socialism etc.

Idealism:

While exploring the various facets of political theory, it would never be prudent to ignore idealism which once upon a time was popular and at the same time formed an important part of political theory. Idealism was first explained and vigorously argued by Plato and Aristotle and later on it received elaborate treatment at the hands of German philosophers, Kant (1724-1804), Hegel (1770-1831) and Fichte (1762- 1814) and Oxford idealists. Idealism is opposed to empiricism. The doctrine propounds that knowledge and sense cannot be derived from experience but from thought.

Idealism also believes that certain eternal values and principles are of vital importance and they have developed through ages and their evolution has reached a stage which cannot be questioned and challenged. These values and principles are manifested in the state to which the individuals must display absolute obedience.

It also preaches that individuals are basically rational and they want fuller blossoming of the values, ideals, ethical and moral principles and according to idealism, this ambitious objective can be achieved through the membership of state. Up to the first half of the nineteenth century, Idealists' philosophy occupied a niche in the whole gamut of political theory. Idealism has various interpretations and versions, but the mere fact is that its association with political theory is a fait accompli.

Nationalism:

The involvement of nationalism with political theory may be contested by many, but a scrutiny of the various aspects of political theory reveals that its association with political theory cannot be ruled out. The nationalist feeling, the concept of nation, state, urge for right to self-determination etc. were all very much active behind the emergence of nationalism.

If we look at the history of Western political thought we shall find that in the fields of nationalism and nation state Machiavelli was the pioneer. In The Prince he advised the prince to unify the various parts of Italy by any means and to establish a nation-state. In fact, nationalism or nation-state per se help flourish the political theory, but its multi faceted developments helped political theory to thrive and one such facet is the concept of sovereignty.

The indomitable urge of the industrialised nations of Europe to dominate the vast territories of Africa and Asia inflamed the nationalist feeling of the people of Asia and Africa. Almond and Powell have rightly observed that in the first-half of the twentieth century, there was a clear absence of political theory and political developments that took place in the Third world states.

These developments were the outcomes of nationalism. This leads to the birth of comparative politics. However, the fact is that the rise and development of nationalism have assisted the progress of political theory. Today comparative politics is an integral part of political theory and their integration has enriched political science to a considerable extent.

Modern Period: Empiricism:

Factors Contributing to the Emergence of Empiricism:

After the Second World War (1939-1945) some top ranking political thinkers of America took a venture to explain the subject by borrowing techniques from different science subjects. This attempt laid the foundation of a new approach to the study of political science.

In the second place, the rapid advance of Marxism in the first few decades of the twentieth century and particularly after the Bolshevik Revolution (1917) in Russia created panic in the minds of political scientists and educationists. The main cause of the panic was that the rapid advance of Marxism and socialist thought was about to expose the real picture of capitalism which was exploitative in nature. To the protagonists of capitalism this was a potent cause of anxiety and tension.

They apprehended that socialism might dethrone capitalism from its present position. All of them decided to combat this situation in an academic way. They thought that a confidence should be created in the minds of people that liberal political thought was much superior to Marxism and in order to do that liberal political analysis must be based on scientific methods and this mentality created a tremendous impact upon the way of explaining the subject.

Thirdly, in the 1940s, a good number of scholars and political scientists from Europe migrated to America and their intention was to introduce new methods of analysis. This point has been aptly pointed out by a critic in the following way, "Beginning in the 1940s, the basic values of American political science were fundamentally challenged by an ideologically diverse group of emigre scholars who coalesced around the project of initiating the first root and branch critique of the discipline".

All of them defended that the discipline must be explained scientifically. This strong determination brought sea changes in the methods of analysis and the fact is that the attempt brought good results.

Fourthly, the Cold War and other connected factors stressed upon science. It was believed in those days that only a proper cultivation of science could yield good and desirable results. Scholars and educationists of USA began to perceive science not simply as an end but also a means and the means would be used to achieve perfection or improvement. Scientists invested their energy and genius to make war weapons more destructive. Political scientists wanted to improve the method of analysis.

Another reason is the traditional political theory for long periods of time revolved around norms and values which means that political science is a normative science. Its emphasis on "is" and "ought" was so important and the penchant for that emphasis made political theory unattractive. Many scholars decided to improve the methods of analysis. Just at that time the Rockefeller Foundation launched a project to facilitate the research of mass communication and American Political Science Association came forward to take this lucrative opportunity.

The purpose was to lay the foundation of a "value-free operational language of political enquiry and as an exercise in scientific political theory". The Rockefeller foundation wanted thorough and fruitful research on the conflict between liberal political theory and the Bolshevik or Marxist approach to political theory.

It also wanted to make a thorough inquiry on war, famine, atomic destruction and their collective impact upon the study of political theory. Two important alternatives appeared before the researchers—to scrupulously adhere to the traditional value added political theory or to posit the theory on scientific foundation and the second alternative finally triumphed. From the 1950s we witness the triumphant advance of empirical analysis of political theory.

Postmodernism:

Another offshoot of modern political theory is post-modernism. It is difficult to define this concept precisely. Since the 1950s political theory was embraced by a new phenomenon which is called postmodernism. It implies that there is nothing like certainty, absolute and universal truth. The whole world is changing as well as outlook and behaviour of individuals and in such situation nothing can be fixed or permanent. It emphasizes on discourse, debate and democracy.

The important feature of postmodernism is that "it stands for the end of science, the death of history, the elimination of objectivity and the very idea of truth, the denial of the world of things and events, the end of cause and effect". Another critic has put the concept in the following words, "As a tool of social and political analysis postmodernism highlights the shift away from societies structured by industrialisation and class solidarity to increasingly fragmented and pluralistic information societies".

We thus see that postmodernism believes in atomic individualism. In its opinion individual is the only final determiner of everything. It denies the authority. But post modernism is silent about anarchism. However, its view leads to anarchist structure of society.

Rational Choice Theory:

Origin and Central Idea:

In the fifties and sixties of the last century political theory witnessed a new development in its own arena and it is popularly known as rational choice theory. In modern time the theory found its roots in the analysis of Hobbes who said that society with a government of absolute powers far better than state of nature. Here is a clear choice of individuals. Because of certain deficiencies people preferred civil society to state of nature.

There are clear hints of the theory in the writings of other thinkers. The rational choice theory originated in Anthony Dawn's noted book An Economic Theory of Democracy (1957). Duncan Black published The Theory of Committee and Elections in 1958. Herbert Simon's Models of Man was published in 1957. Between 1957 and 1973 there were published a number of books which deal with rational choice.

The central idea of the doctrine is when a man or group of men are given a number of alternatives they, after calculating all the aspects, decide a particular course of action. That is, they arrive at a decision. Behind the arrival of the decision rationality of the person concerned plays a vital role. In other words, rationality is the chief guiding force and because of this it is called rational choice theory.

By the mid-1970s the theory was very popular and it was first applied to economics and then political scientists took interest. Hence the central idea of the rational choice theory of politics is reason or rationality is the main determiner of people's choice. Moved by rationality men select an action.

Features of the Theory:

From what has been said by its proponents certain features can be derived. One such feature is there is an identifiable set of actions which lead to an identifiable set of outcomes or results of these actions. Here the word identifiable is very important. Both actions and outcomes can be identified. In the second place the participants in the actions are rational and reasonable and they can order the preferences considering outcome. They can identify the actions and at the same time the consequences.

This enables them to take a particular course of action. In the third place, several alternatives are placed before the participants or actors and they are given the freedom to choose any one of the alternatives. In the fourth place, the actors or participants select that alternative which can assure the maximum benefit or utility.

In the fifth place, while selecting the alternative the actor applies his intelligence or reason so that he can arrive at a comfortable or viable position. In the sixth place, the rational choice model assures that while going to select a particular alternative the individual is not faced with any restriction the meaning of which is he enjoys full freedom.

Finally, the rational choice model starts with the individual level and reaches the collective level. That is, from micro level to macro level. The rational choice level is the hyphen between micro and macro levels.

Assessment:

The rational choice theory has been subjected to a number of criticisms. It gives emphasis on alternatives and their outcomes. The problem is what is the exact number of the alternatives and their outcomes? The advocates of the theory cannot throw light on this issue and this creates confusion and deficiency.

The supporters of the theory claim that it can help the researchers to arrive at a fruitful discussion of politics and political theory will get inspiration from it. But critics are of opinion that since the back bone of the theory is rationality this very rationality can be questioned. How many individuals possess the rationality?

Heywood observes: "In proceeding from an abstract model of individual, rational choice theory pays insufficient attention to social and historical factors". There is another objection. For the proper functioning of the theory a liberal or democratic set up of the society is essential.

All the individuals or at least the rational persons will be given sufficient freedom to select the most desirable alternatives so that he/she can maximise his/her utility or benefit. But such an atmosphere is not easily available. It is alleged that the doctrine may effectively work at the micro level, but its success at the macro level is not encouraging at all.

A clash of interest, choices and tastes is inevitable and how is an equilibrium to be attained? Its advocates cannot assure us on this issue. There is still a limitation of the theory. For the development of rationality or reason education and favourable circumstances are required which are not easily available.

The Task of Political Theory:

We have very briefly surveyed the revival or resurgence of political theory in the 1950s and 1960s. A pertinent question which peeps into our mind is why a large number of political scientists and researchers took so much trouble and time to do the research work for the resurgence of political theory? The answer to this vexed question lies in the importance or task of political theory.

Almond, Powell, David Easton, Robert Dahl, Lasswell and Kaplan etc. took special care in regard to the comprehensive analysis of political system which the traditional thinkers avoided. Easton says: "For a variety of reasons a theoretical frame work is essential to an adequate analysis of political system". Only a systematic and well-built theory is capable of identifying the important political variables and analysing the relations among them.

In the second place, according to Easton a political theory "maps out the areas in which additional or new research is badly needed". Finally, a political theory "adds to the reliability of the results of both new and old research in a way impossible without the existence of a relatively consistent body of concepts".

The function of a political theory (some critics call general theory though there is difference between the two), is to construct a conceptual framework through which to make sense of disparate phenomena.

Classification of Political Theory:

Value Theory and Causal Theory:

The political scientists of the second half of the twentieth century were quite conscious of the importance of theory and remembering this they framed a structure of political theory. Easton says that a theory is used to mean many things. In the first place according to Easton a theory is used for explaining the values or philosophical aspects of politics.

Here the word value is used not in the sense of economics, but in philosophical or moral or ethical sense. In cases more than one theory is used to indicate value. Easton calls it Value Theory. We can say value comprises a part of political theory and in that sense it is called Value Theory.

There is a second type of theory designated by Easton and it called Causal Theory. A causal theory is one which is used to find out a relation between facts. The researcher collects facts and tries to find out relationship among them and while doing so in his mind there is always a picture of theory which is quite active.

Easton points out the importance of causal theory in the following words: "The importance of causal theory lies in the fact that it is an index of the stage of development of any science, social or physical, towards the attainment of reliable knowledge. Very briefly, causal theory is a device for improving the dependability of our knowledge".

Factual Theory:

For building up of a theory, it is essential that facts are to be collected and analysed. But mere collection of facts is not enough, their analysis is also important and for that purpose theoretical knowledge is also essential. Before entering into a detailed analysis we want to define facts and we shall do it in the words of Easton: "A fact is a particular ordering of reality in terms of a theoretical interest".

But the collection of facts or data like a blind man is not enough. While collecting data or facts sufficient intelligence and knowledge are to be applied because only with the help of facts and data we can build up the foundation of a theory. When a researcher collects facts and data, he carries with him a clear picture and frame of a theory and on the basis of that, he starts his work of collecting facts. For this reason, Easton says—"Facts therefore imply duty".

In Easton's analysis of factual theory, we further observe that facts and data are to be collected with a good deal of acumen and after that two functions are to be performed. One is the relationship among the data is to be established and the other is facts and data are to be generalised. "Every generalisation," Easton continues, "is in a sense a theory, it is a statement of relationship which is only probably, not certainly and finally, true". Facts and data are to be critically examined.

Three Propositions:

Easton discusses the political theory in the light of behaviouralism. He is of opinion that though there are differences in the political behaviour of individuals, a close observation reveals that there are also uniformities in the political behaviour and on the basis of those uniformities the political scientists form generalisations and theory. Easton points out three such forms. One is Singular Generalisation. Second is Narrow Gauge theory and the third is Broad Gauge theory.

In Easton's opinion, the Singular Generalisations are not in the strict sense theories. The researcher collects uniform behaviour of individuals and after analysing them prepares at certain conclusions or we can say he forms generalisations. Easton calls it singular generalisations.

The political scientist analyses very few variables and on the basis of that he forms generalisations. This approach is not a sufficient way of framing an acceptable theory. Singular generalisations are the primary level of a political theory and it is not surprising that he does not call it a political theory.

At the higher level there is a Narrow Gauge Theory. It is also called Synthetic Theory. In the words of Easton the narrow gauge theory "consists of a set of interrelated propositions that are designed to synthesise the data contained in an unorganised body of singular generalisations".

The supporters of the narrow gauge theory are accustomed to viewing political theory and political science in terms of power enunciated by Lasswell. He viewed political science as simply the study of the struggle of or for power. According to Lasswell, in any society there are various groups and consequently many centres of power. Each group or each centre always tries to capture power by defeating the other group.

This is particularly the characteristic feature of any pluralist society. According to Lasswell and several others, power always remains at the centre of any political analysis because no society can be analysed without power. The narrow gauge theory, no doubt, is broader than the singular generalisation, but it is not really broad because power can never be the central theme of a theory.

Finally, there is a Broad Gauge Theory. It can also be called Systematic Theory. Hierarchically viewed broad gauge theory is at the highest stage of the whole series. It is neither narrow nor singular. In the considered judgment of Easton in any society there occur large number of incidents and facts and all these are not relevant for any political scientist. Only few or selective facts or data may be useful for him.

Here the problem is how he will select these facts and data? Before a political scientist starts to collect and analyse data and facts he forms a conceptual framework and this acts as a guidance. The conceptual framework is a kind of sieve which selects data and facts.

Status of Political Theory:

We have already noted that the gravest charge against the traditional political theory is—it is extremely reluctant to apply improved and sophisticated methods of other - sciences, particularly natural sciences. If the traditional political theory could do that it would have been able to improve its status as a branch of science subjects such as economics and psychology.

Many serious persons and policy-makers refuse to put political science or political theory, economics, psychology and several other subjects within the same bracket. It is lamented that since political scientists do not use sophisticated data, its conclusions have failed to satisfy many.

Easton says that political theory as well as political science has not been able to establish itself as a distinct branch of social science. In earlier epochs, large number of persons associated with the disciplines treated it as a branch of history or economics and this was never a matter of prestige for political scientists.

It has been observed that this lower status of political theory or political science was chiefly due to the reason that it was not able to draw the attention of serious scholars and researchers. But Easton claims that "Political Science does constitute a distinct field of research, not for problems of application alone, but, what is more significant, for analytical and conceptual purposes as well".

For the enhancement of status, utility, importance, etc. of a discipline it is essential that it (the discipline) must construct a theoretical framework and political theory up to the fifties has not been able to do that. Easton concludes that political science must accept that venture boldly.

Again, prediction is an important function of a science subject. Subjects of social science in general and political science in particular are not always able to make proper predictions. But that drawback must not be over-emphasized. Political Theory can be elevated to that status and for that purpose, political theory must be made a comprehensive theory.

Let us again quote Easton. "Where research has been quantitatively and qualitatively adequate to permit of prediction its success is geared neatly to the existence of a comprehensive body of consistent theory". If a comprehensive and consistent theory exists prediction becomes feasible.

Easton's main point is that to enable political theory to make prediction its research work must be improved and must be made a distinct discipline. During the first half of the twentieth century, there was a lot of resentment in the academic world of political science in America because of the inadequacy of research in this subject. A large number of political scientists have however been able to change it.

In conclusion few words may be added. If we go through the various concepts, approaches and models prepared by the political scientists we shall witness an interesting fact. Time has not yet arrived to say anything about the subject (political science) assertively. The excessive stress on values, judgment and norms was challenged by empiricists. Again in the seventies there has occurred a revival of traditionalism and it is highly prominent in Rawls' analysis of justice.

In his revised version of behaviouralism (which is popularly knows post-behaviouralism), Easton argued in favour of values and norms. Postmodernism puts a challenge to both traditionalism and empiricism. It claims that there is not such thing as absolute or universal truth, norms and values. It even challenges the social and economic structure of society based on industrialisation.

From 1950s to 1990s, people renewed their faith on socialism but the collapse of the erstwhile Soviet Union has destroyed that faith.

Theorizing the 'Political'

Without trying to attempt a precise definition of the nature and scope of Political Science, one might say that there is a "broad" view and a "narrow" view of politics and political phenomena – the one placing its main emphasis on political functions and treating politics as a process or a type of activity and the other on political structures and orienting itself towards various types of political institutions. Aristotle was clearly taking a broad view of politics, when he searched for it not only in the state, but also in the family, the corporation, the association or the church, whereas the discussion of politics in the subsequent centuries was limited, by and large, to its narrow view, which interpreted politics as the study of the political and the governmental sub-systems of society. We find the contemporary writers, like Catin, once again breaking away from this narrow view and emphasising the phenomenal struggle for control as their central concern. With the emergence of this view, political scientists are no longer satisfied with merely descriptive categories, though accurate description is a necessary first step to other steps, but would like to take up more refined and sophisticated techniques of analysis. They would like to convert, in other words, what was regarded as political philosophy or political thought or political theory into political science. Catlin, for example, would think of political science as "indistinguishable – on any intellectually respectable grounds from sociology" and maintain that the sociologists' study of "myriads of individual acts and thousands of relations between groups" afforded the basis "for authentic comparisons and in the best tradition of Aristotle and Machiavelli for the observation of constants". One might, however, wonder whether a concept of politics which included the family control system and the ecclesiastical polity was not so broad as to be meaningless and think that it might perhaps be better to strike a balance between the two extreme views.

CHAPTER III

Traditions of Political Theory: Liberal, Marxist, Anarchist and Conservative

Approaches to the Study of Political Theory – Liberal, Conservative Traditions

Introduction

In political theory, numerous theories and traditions have been developed to analyse and comprehend politics. Each method has essential premises and postulates that define it. But they are all diverse and influenced by various traditions. This presentation provides an overview of two important political theories: liberalism and conservatism. Political theory is a set of political interpretations (Gaus 2000: 47). In this process, political theory strives to connect concepts (such liberty and equality) in novel ways. Gaus (2000) mentions three "enduring political theories": liberalism, socialism, and conservatism. Gaus stresses that they are not monoliths; each method has tremendous variability. Alan Ryan's idea of "liberalisms" is worth mentioning (Ryan 2007). All of these traditions have a wide range of differences, yet they all share a set of 'foundations' that define them apart. That is, certain characteristics distinguish each of them.

Liberalism

Waldron (2004) says that liberals share family affinities but have opposing value conceptions. But these affinities constitute solid liberal foundations. Indeed, liberals have endeavoured to distinguish liberalism from conservatism and socialism (see Gaus 2000; Ryan 2007). But many define liberalism differently. The commitment to liberty is a feature Gaus sees in all branches of liberalism (Gaus 2000: 46). However, John Gray (1995) describes liberalism's defining element as modern perspective of man (person) and society. But, across all liberal strands,

Individualist, egalitarian, universalist, and meliorist are four modernist concepts, according to Gray. Liberalism is an individualist philosophy; egalitarianism is liberalism's claim to moral equality; universalism is liberalism's belief in the improbability of institutions and social arrangements; and meliorism is a core liberal tradition feature (Gray 1995: xii). John Locke's Second Treatise on Civil

Government was the "crystallisation" of liberalism, according to Gray. Lockean liberty is based on freedom of association, private property, and limited government. In a separate vein, Vincent (2009: 25) claims liberalism stems from a constitutionalist tradition in 19th century Europe.

The liberal approach to political thought is founded on fundamental principles.

• Gray claims a liberal perspective is universalism. Liberals do not represent any single interest group or portion of the population (see Gray 1995). Liberals posed their demands not as those of a particular group, but as those of all humanity.

To approach liberal political theory, rationality, autonomy, and choice are variables. Liberalism is therefore a non-teleological approach to politics and life. A liberal approach, unlike Greek political thought, does not pursue the idea of a telos or final end; the idea of good life and society is a matter of individual choice. Also, liberals favour a 'thin' common good over a 'thick' common good of communitarians (Kymlicka 2001). For example, in liberal traditions, individuals voluntarily participate into a compact that forms society and state. This principle underpins the state and civil society. To explain welfarism, liberals must now reconcile deontic and utilitarian logics (see Gray 1995). To exercise autonomy and self-realization, Gray claims that the welfare logic advocates for making certain resources, powers, or skills available, reinforcing individualism. In A Theory of Fairness (1971), John Rawls focuses on deontological persons entering into social contracts from behind the 'veil of ignorance' to construct a society based on justice and welfare for all. Individuals choose the concepts of justice, not their social and cultural identities.

Most observers see liberalism as a capitalist worldview. In this view, liberalism is defined by private property (see Macpherson 1962). This method may be observed in liberal works from Locke in the 17th century to Hayek, Friedman, Buchanan, and Nozick today. For libertarians like Nozick and Hayek, taxation is a violation of freedom and individuality.

• Individualism may be at the heart of all liberalisms (see Gray 1995; Vincent 2009). In fact, Vincent contends that liberalism's 'ontological core' is individualism (Vincent 2009: 32). Individualism in liberal thought is characterised by a priori individualism, which means that the person is antecedent to society, naturally or morally. But liberal individualism is a difficult ideology. John Dewey distinguishes between 'old liberalism' and 'new liberalism' based on a more socially rooted person. In T. H. Green's view, society can help individuals achieve self-realization (see Vincent 2009: 36). Similarly, society's 'organised effort' is crucial for individual self-direction (Hobhouse, in Vincent 2009: 36). Abstract individualism is not a reality, according to Hayek's market liberalism. Hayek distinguishes between rationalistic individualism (e.g. J.S. Mill) and real individualism (e.g. Hayek is an individualist. On another level, liberalism has seen 'possessive individualism', which holds that an individual owns their body, wants, and interests, as in Locke, Gray, and Nozick. Property is also fundamental in possessive individualism, as it extends bodily rights (see Vincent 2009: 37).

• Liberty is a basic liberal value. Michael Freeden argues that while liberty is a core liberal value, liberal academia has no united perspective on it (Freeden, in Vincent 2009: 37). Liberalism also specifies the scope of state action; liberals favour a limited state where individuals are shielded from state arbitrariness by their rights-bearing status. However, liberalism is divided on the state, with classical liberal, laissez-faire, welfare, and neoliberal states being the most common. 1 A typical liberal distinction is between negative and positive liberty. Whereas negative liberty connotes freedom from limitations or compulsion, positive liberty connotes the ability to exercise freedom. Isaiah Berlin and Friedrich Hayek argue that poverty and unemployment are not restrictions or coercion. Deliberate action is a positive power, according to Green, Laski, and more recently Taylor2.

• Liberalism is committed to rights and democracy. While the Lockean tradition argues for natural rights, the utilitarian reasoning emphasises the legal basis of every right. Liberalism is closely linked to the value of democracy, albeit new definitions of democracy such as robust democracy, unitary democracy, and deliberative democracy have been developed recently.

Deliberately chosen conditions of human flourishing rather than predetermined by society or state are central to a liberal political theory. This explains the liberal-democratic-market alliance. Individuality replaces societal collectivity as the fulcrum of liberalism. For example, a liberal will oppose any arrangement or policy that restricts individual freedom, even if it benefits the whole. Examples are liberal-communitarian debates.

Conservatism

Conservatism, by definition, conserves. In a tone akin to a political dogma, it repeatedly declared itself opposed to change (Honderich 2005:6). Conservatism is thus a political tradition that opposes or is cautious of change; conservatism is characterised by preserving the existing order. Contrary to popular belief, conservatism did not mature until Edmund Burke's turbulent response to the French Revolution (Quinton 2007: 291). Rather, Vincent (2009: 56) traces conservatism back to the fourteenth century. Vincent accepts the mediaeval roots of twentieth century conservative writers. One example is Russell Kirk's conservative heritage extending back to mediaeval city guardians.

Andrew Vincent (2009) explains the multiplicity of conservative technical usages in five positions:

• After the French Revolution, aristocracy negative doctrine. Conservatism is seen as a passing historical phase in European societies from 1790 to 1914. For example, the Tory Party in England developed from late 18th century to 1832.

• A second approach describes conservatism as a political pragmatism that simply absorbs the dominant political, cultural, and moral ethos.

An institutionalised political doctrine's defensive posture is reflected in a third view, situational or positional (Vincent 2009: 58). This conservatism has no socioeconomic, historical or ideological roots. Just like every other institution that upholds the established order. Conservatives exist in liberalism and Marxism.

• Conservatism is also seen as a temperament. Hugh Cecil's "natural conservatism" - a human predisposition to resist change - is one example (ibid). Conservatism is a human propensity to adhere to tried and true views and behaviours.

• Another dispositional view distinguishes reasoning types. Michael Oakeshott is a good example. On one level, this view convinces us that conservatism opposes abstract reasoning and presents reasons why it should (see Vincent 2009: 58).

• Finally, conservatism is seen as an ideology, a set of prescriptive principles. The conservatism of Edmund Burke is exemplified in his works (ibid). Burke questioned the French Revolution's uniqueness in emphasising equality and human perfection through reason and institutional reform.

Vincent also distinguishes three ways to conservatism research: historical nation state, chronological, and conceptual. According to the historical nation state paradigm, conservatism is historical. Noel O'Sullivan and Karl Mannheim both agree that separate British, German, French, and other nation state and history based conservatisms exist. Conservatism is classified chronologically, with each phase defined by a prominent personality and the circumstances of the moment. So British Conservatism begins with Robert Peel, then Disraeli, MacMillan, and Thatcherism. Second, the conceptual perspective ignores the existence of multiple conservatisms. There are many philosophies, but no pure conservatism. Antony Quinton and Roger Scruton agree. The second strand sees conservatism as a whole.

On the right are the New Right (Vincent 2009) and the traditionalists (Vincent 2009).

Traditionalism, scepticism about political knowledge, and the organic notion of humans and society are all interconnected, according to Anthony Quinton (2007). In politics, traditionalism "supports

change, especially sudden large-scale change, and especially violent and systematic revolutionary change" (Quinton 2007: 286). "Conservatives accept change as required by changing circumstances, but they insist that it be continuous and gradual" (ibid: 288). According to Ted Honderich (2005: 9), conservatism prefers reform over change. Change affects something's underlying nature or substance, whereas reform simply affects what is external or accidental (ibid: 10). Furthermore, conservatives like Michael Oakeshott argue for keeping traditions because society is familiar with them (see Honderich 2005: 17). As Noel O'Sullivan points out, what defines change/reform and indeed conservatism in different communities may be different. Reform is not predetermined; conservatism might range from defensive efforts to pushing changes to maintain status quo (Honderich 2005: 22). Extending suffrage to the Whigs was an example of the former.

This casts a dark shadow over conservatism. Changes bring both good and terrible outcomes. Their pessimism towards 'progress' stems from the fact that development has negative consequences. Many have described conservatism as the 'politics of imperfection' (see Quinton 2007). Kekes (2004) interprets this flaw differently. According to Kekes, conservatism likewise assumes the human situation is fine. Human nature is a mix of good and evil, yet both individuals and societies have limited control over it (Kekes 2004: 139). Unlike liberals, conservatives believe humans are not rational machines, but rather a complicated network of emotions, thoughts, and impulses (Vincent 2009: 68). This validates their cynicism in human reformation, which Peter Viereck described as the 'political secularisation of original sin' (Vincent 2009: 69).

In conservatism, tradition mediates between individual autonomy and societal authority to construct a desirable life:

A tradition is a set of customary ideas, behaviours, and acts that have lasted and engendered loyalty among people. A tradition might be reflective and planned, like the Supreme Court's discussions, or unreflective and..... It's not just religious or horticultural or scientific or athletic or political or stylistic or moral or artistic. They are everywhere (Kekes 2004: 136).

That example, a person's idea of a decent life is to follow the traditions passed down through history. Individual autonomy and social authority are thus reconciled in conservative ideas through autonomous participation in social traditions. Likewise, conservatism opposes customs that defy basic human requirements (see Kekes 2004). So who chooses these customs? Conservatives argue that decisions should be made by those properly empowered by the political process; decisions should be made based on the tradition's historical contribution to society; positive contributions should be kept; negative contributions should be rejected. Conservatism is thus a logical and reflective defence of durable established structures (see Kekes 2001; Honderich 2005).

(2) Experience and established institutions and practises embody political knowledge. So conservatism opposes utopias and systemic change initiatives (ibid). Third, conservatism rejects the idea of a universal human nature. Human nature, therefore, changes from time to time and place to place due to organic relations between individuals and society. The conservative viewpoint is that natural science abstractions or theories cannot evolve. Quinton argues that conservatism is procedural or technical rather than substantive as an ideology. It

imposes no universal principles, values, or institutions, and hence violates its own rejection of abstract theory" (Quinton 2007: 288). Conservatives support abstract theory because of Burke's contrast between abstraction (metaphysical reason) and custom and tradition. In Oakeshott's case, practical knowledge trumped logical technical knowledge. This renders conservatism antagonistic to utopias, social contracts, and abstract concepts like rights (see Quinton 2007; Kekes 2004). Rather, they use their own society's history to shape their present and future (Kekes 2004). Politics should be based on history:

Conservatives agree that history is a good place to start, but they believe it is not a coincidence that certain political arrangements have historically benefited people while others have not (Kekes 2004: 131).

Consequently, conservatism is based on a moral order in history, and thus political morality (Kekes 2004).

Instead of philosophical or utopian concerns, history is likely to reveal meaningful considerations for or against the political arrangements that are possible in that society (Kekes 2004: 135).

Third, conservatism is based on an organic, hierarchical view of society. Only the organic whole can explain the individual. Society is thus a network of interrelated pieces, not an artifice or mechanism as liberals claim. As a result, political order evolves from existing moral and political institutions. Except for the New Right in conservatism, political leadership and skill are reserved for a few few. For example, Burke called political power a natural aristocracy (see Vincent 2009). Why do conservatives hate democracy? Conservatives favour restricted democracy, such Edmund Burke's "virtual representation." 3 Because human nature is flawed, government must offer a framework of procedures and norms. Freedom, rights, liberty, and property are not moral principles; they serve the community's objectives (ibid). Except for the New Right and more liberal conservatives, conservatism is defined by a hierarchically regulated society but a free market economy. Finally, the conservative tradition is also defined by its resistance to theory. Conservatism contends that no social theory can encompass the intricacies of society. It is a folly therefore to apply theory to society (Honderich 2005: 32). (Honderich 2005: 32). Russell Kirk's rejection of a priori conceptions as separated from history and circumstances is an example (see Kirk, in Honderich 2005). (see Kirk, in Honderich 2005). Similarly, Oakseshott's repudiation of rationalism in politics is another confirmation of conservatism's break from Enlightenment reasoning, moral philosophy and social engineering (ibid: 34). (ibid: 34). This has often been described as conservatism's anti-ideology (see Vincent 2009). (see Vincent 2009). Honderich (2005) contends that the conviction of conservatism in time tested traditions and experiences implies that it denounces philosophical abstractions and promotes a form of empiricism.

Anarchist

Anarchism in the 20th century was marked by a strong paradox: The first half of the century saw the golden age of anarchist thought and action, with anarchists playing important roles and making substantial political gains from Asia to Europe to North America. The second half of the century, on the other hand, saw the retreat of anarchist thought into the margins of political struggles, with 'anarchism' in the public eye largely becoming a synonym for a complete lack of order and aimless chaos and violence. Much of this latter development can be explained by the bipolar world of the Cold War era and the stark division of the global political order between capitalist democracies and state-socialisms, both of which saw anarchism as a threat to their institutionalized order.

At the turn of the century, anarchist movements across the globe inherited a strong heritage of political action. Anarchists were present across the political spectrum, from violent political action to philosophy and literature. While anarchist labor organizations were notable parts of the global struggles for the five-day workweek and eight-hour workday (from the previous seven days of 12 to 14 hours of work), other anarchists took to violence and yet others published and agitated. Anarchists killed kings, nobles, presidents and parliamentarians (for instance, the Italian anarchist Gaetano Bresci shot and killed King Umberto of Italy in 1900; in 1901, the American anarchist Leon Czolgosz shot and killed US President William McKinley). In the philosophical realm, anarchism was making splashes as well: one of the most influential anarchists of the time, Peter Kropotkin, who was once a Russian Prince and aid to the Tzar before stepping down for his ideals, published his "Mutual Aid" in 1902. Anarchist communes and groups played major roles in numerous uprisings in Europe and beyond. Following the First World War in particular, widespread disillusionment with the economic and political systems further fueled anarchist movements and even gave rise to the world's first anarchist territory in Ukraine. Anarchists also had a major presence in the Spanish Civil War and resisted the fascist takeover alongside communist forces. As could be expected, anarchists were present in all resistance movements fighting the Nazi occupation and they even formed loosely organized guerilla forces throughout Europe.

The relatively stable bipolar world order following the Second World War left little room for anarchism as both poles – authoritarian communism and liberal capitalism – fought to silence alternative ideologies. Despite a concerted effort from the world's superpowers, however, anarchist communes blossomed wherever they could find room, from the freed territories in Denmark, to Kibbutzim in Israel, to communes in San Francisco. Anarchism, however, ceased to be perceived as a major world ideology and was demoted in the public eye to disorganized chaos and meaningless violence. In the absence of diminished militantism and direct political action, literary anarchism became the main stream of anarchist presence continuing a strong tradition of anarchistic education theory (like the Ferrer and Moderna schools). Thinkers and writers such as Robert Paul Wolff, John Simmons and James C. Scott have been prolific in arguing the case of anarchy in history, philosophy and political science.

Following the collapse of the Soviet Union, it seemed, momentarily, that capitalist liberal democracies had won the day. Disillusionment soon followed, however and faced with tremendous economic inequality and collapsing ecological systems, anarchistic communes and movements are resurfacing throughout the globe. Workers' collectives, associations, syndicates, anti-fascist organizations, climate justice movements, feminist and LGBTQI+ movements and even local electoral politics have become fertile grounds for social anarchists seeking to engage in direct political action. Indeed, compared to a few decades ago, it is safe to say that anarchists and anarchism are making a strong and visible comeback.

Marxist

Karl Marx the profounder of Marxism was a revolutionary thinker. He tried to bring a revolution in the world. Like other writers he did not merely explain the circumstances of his time but forth a plan to change
them. He said that the other philosopher have sought to interpret the world. What matters however is to change it. Marx was in favor of raising a new society on debris of the wall one in his opinion the state is an oppressive

organization which protects property and which, with the help of power, protects the interests of the capitalist. He criticized the various aspects of liberalism very vehemently and he proved this idea of liberalism wrong that with the help of state and politics peace order and justice will be established in the world that with the help of power protects the interests of the capitalists. He criticized the various aspects of liberalism very vehemently and he proved this idea of liberalism wrong that with the help of state and politics were the means to make the rule of the rich stable. Harmony and cooperation were not possible with the help of state. It only creates conflict interpreting the point of view of Marx, M. Duverger says, "Politics is conflict a struggle in which power allows those who posses it to ensure, their hold on society and profit by it."

1. Material Condition are the basic of politics: According to Marx the basic of politics are material condition. Material condition here means the modes of production. He has clarified that there was not state or politics in primitive age of communism because modes of production were very simple at that time and there was no conflict. But when there was a change in the material condition settle the form of politics also. Thus material condition settle the form of politics also. Thus the material condition are the basic of politics which give directions to human behavioral.
Marx and Engels wrote both social and political institutions must be regarded as outgrowths of material condition which direct major paths of human behavior.

2. Politics is the study of class struggle: According to Marx, politics comes into being when there are two oppositese classes in the society because conflict between these two opposites classes in the society. Thus, this constantly going on conflict is studied as politics. He says that in the primitive society because of absence of these opposite classes there was no politics after the primitive society till today the conflict between the two classes has been going on constantly and it will go on accounting to Marx till the final stage of this conflict i.e. the establishment of a classes society. Thus we call the study of conflict of these two mutually opposing classes produced by material conditions as politics.

3. According to Marxists state and politics depends on social condition of man and with the changes in social conditions, the form of the state and politics also change. Thus, Marx also admits that politics is aspect of social process.

4. To Marx, the subject is always a social man: While studying the liberal view of politics, we saw that they recognized separate authorities of the individual and social and they say that the society should be used for the development of the individual. That is why stronger liberals felt that the authority of state makes the individual more and more slavish. They advocate a limited sphere of the state by calling it a necessary evil. But the later liberals, when they wanted the welfare to state. To when they wanted the welfare of the individual through state, wanted to state. Thus, according to the liberals the relations of the individual with state is only to the extent to which it fulfills interests of the individual.

5. Marx followed the ideal of Aristotle and Hegal in relation to individual can be considered only as a social being. The individual and society being. The individual and society are neither separate nor their interest separate. Discussing this point of view of Marx, Lefebvre says in his "The sociology of Marx" "To Marx subject is always a social man, the individual viewed in his actual relationship with groups, classes, society as a whole."

Marx considered individual as a part of society to cover the gulf between the individual and the society in a capitalists set up and for full development of the individual. In the capitalists set up and for full development of the individual. In the capitalists set up man is a properties man and in it propertied man in it there is exploitation of man by man. Marx wanted lired to build society. Marx wanted to demolished the wall of property between the individual and the society. It will make the establishment of society based on equality possible.

6. All political conflict are class conflicts: By giving materialistic into predations of history, Marx tried to prove that, after the primitive stage, there have been two mutually opposing classes on the basic of material condition of the society. The form of these classes is determined by modes of production of the time. He says that material condition are basic of all social relations are the struggle for between two mutually opposing classes based on economic interests.

7. Marx disagree with the traditional interpretation of politics in which polities is related to the political and ethical questions. He said that the form of all types of politics struggle of indirectly class struggle which can be seen in the capitalists countries. Though the struggle are indirectly class struggle as the study of history indicates. Thus all the struggle going on in the state, means of production are owned by it. It exploits the proletariat class and uses all materials resources for the satisfaction of interests, politics is their means with the help of which the help of which they exploit the working class. Marx calls it anti-polities and false politics.

8. Politics creates consciousness in the proletariat. According to Marx main function of politics is to create consciousness in the individual which helps in bringing change in the society. He says that, by reading history, it becomes clear that society is dynamic, but this change is brought through conflict which helps between the opposing economic interests.

Marx says that before the revolution which establishment dictatorship of the proletariat, the main junction of politics is to bring such consciousness among workers which may encourage them to struggle with the capitalists. Lenin has said that the working class takes part in politics to bring change in society. The more, he is active in politics, the more conscious he becomes about class confict. This process will give labourers to establish their dictatorship through revolution. Thus according to the communist ideology, before the revolution, politics, perform function of creating conscious for revolution. Thus according to the communist ideology, before the revolution, politics perform function of creating conscious for revolution.

9. Politics will stamp out the last remnants of capitalism and will be used as a meant for the establishment of a new society. According to Marx, after the revolution brought by the working class, capitalists set up will be destroyed and dictatorship of the proletariat will be established.

Because politics is a process which brings change therefore, after the revolution, during dictatorship of the revolution, during dictatorship of the proletariat will established. Because politics is a process which brings change, therefore, after the revolution, during dictatorship of the proletariat, politics will play an important role, unlike the capitalists set up, politics is no lougher a means of explotiting to the labourers, but it worker for making dictatorship of the proletariat stronger. At this stage, politics, on one hand, destorys the remnants of capitalism and on the other it is used for protecting interests of the labourers. In the transaction stage, politics is not used in the form of play of authority because every body is performed his duty and there is no need of oppression or pressure for it. The whole of the society will be united by the moral principles and social bonds. Thus, the need to of the state will end and it will neither away. According to the Marxists it will be the golden period.

Marx and Engels have not written much about this stage. Perhaps, they were not quite clear about it. They had invisaged a society also politics will not disappear because directions of change and development of classes society also, politics will not disappear because directions of change and development will not half. Development in a classless society will be peaceful in the absence of the class conflict, but there may be contradictions in society at this stage also which may not result in enmity. Function of the politics will be to the solution of these political consciousness in the individual and rational knowledge will grow. Thus in a classless society, politics works in such a way that it generates and develops rational knowledge.

Criticism of the Marxists view of politics

Though, because of the spread of communism there is no dearth of writers who support Marxists view of politics, because of the defect in the Marxists view of politics. That is why, Marxists view has been critically discussed below:

1. The individual-self is merged in the social-self: Idea of Marx about the individual has actually merged the individual-self with the social-self. The fact is that in liberalism, society was so much neglected for the individual that some powerful person of the society fully exploited others, but on the other hand, because of the of the all round development of the individual as a part of society in communism, free personality of the individual was lot merged the self of the individual in the social-self. Thus it may be liberalism or communism, the class, owing the material resources and political power, uses the common man of the society as a means of the fulfillments of its interest. Marxists claim that polities in an instrument of development of the individual, but practically, they use him for the exploitation. This fact becomes clear studying social set up of those countries where dictatorship of the proletariat has been established.

2. Material condition are not the only basic of politics: Marx recognised man only in his economic capacity and he think that the other aspects of his life depends only on material condition. Religious, cultural, moral and others aspects of his life depends only on material condition. Religious, cultural, moral and other sentimental aspects of individual are influenced by his economic life and direction is provided by it. That is why, Marx has come to the conclusion the material condition of man are the basic of politics, but these are not the sole basis. In additional to the cultural, religious, spiritual and moral values, traditions and customs of a country also influenced it's political process. Marx admitted this fact in his later writing and admitted that only economic conditions are not believed to be the whole process of political developments. Clarifying this fact, Fyodorov says, "Marxism Leninism, however does not considered that whole process of political developments is only directly and indirectly dependents on production." Avineri also says that Marx, in his later writing, did not considered politics only as a reflection of the economic conditions. Thus, political process, as explained by Marx, seems to be defective in itself.

3. Politics is not merely the study of class-struggle: Marx has divided into two mutually opposite classes capitalists and labourers. The fact is that every society is divided into two mutually opposite classes capitalists and labourers. The fact is that every society is divided into various classes and those classes are not necessarily organised on economic basis. Some of these classes may be such that they have no economic basis and there is no condition of their being in struggle. Even between the capitalists and the labourers, as explained by Marx these days there is cooperation and not struggle because the labourers and the capitalists as discussed by Marx, do not seem to be working now. So, saying that the politics is merely a study of class struggle is not logical because the form of class struggle does not seem to be working in the society. Politics is an instrument for exploiting the labourers and consequently economic conditions of the labourers will worsen but the study of social organization of capitalists countries that there capitalists class has made many changes and arrangment on the other hand their professional efficiency hand their professional efficiency has increased. It does not prove assertion of Karl Marx that politics will become the basic of economic exploitation in the capitalists countries.

4. Politics also did not create consciousness for revolution: The countries where communist revolution have occurred, were not industrially advanced as Marx had claimed. And, in modern times, no revolution has been brought by the labourers in the industrailised countries. The fact is that because of fulfillment of economic, social and cultural demand and because of betterment in their condition consciousness of class struggle did not develop in the labourers in capitalists countries. So it is clear that in the capitalists society politics does not prepare ground for class struggle.

5. The politics could not becomes a mean to establish a new society. According to Marx, after the revolution, politics will be utilised for destroying remnants of capitalism and to eradicate the traditions and moral values of capitalism and out of it such a society will be established in which there is no place for class struggle. The whole of society will become one class cannot be solved peacefully. According to the Marxists, "The said circumstances present in the society will alive till socialist change the whole society set up through a violent revolution." According to the Marxists, until class struggle of society is destroyed, social co operative cannot be established by ending the conflict only classes society can be a society minus conflict.

CHAPTER IV

Approaches to Political Theory: Normative, Historical and Empirical

It is quite difficult to identify and categorise various conceptions of political theory which are put into use by theorists. The difficulty emanates from a tendency among theorists to go for an exercise in which they start drawing on different conceptions and traditions. This is truer, as we will see later, with contemporary political theory than with the ones which preceded it. In the past, theorists somewhat maintained a purity of conception in theory–building and seldom out stepped the framework they had chosen. But this does not apply to the contemporary times, which are a witness to a crop of theory which appears hybrid in nature. But broadly speaking, three different conceptions emerge in political theory on the basis of which both the past and the present theories can be conceptualised, judged and evaluated. They are: Historical, Normative and Empirical.

Historical Approach

Many theorists have attempted theory – building on the basis of insights and resources from history. Sabine is one of the main exponents of the historical conception. In his opinion, a question such as what is the nature of political theory can be answered descriptively; that is, how theory has responded to historical events and specific situations. In other words, in this perspective, political theory becomes situation dependent in which each historical situation sets a problem, which in turn is taken care of through solutions devised by the theory. This conception of political theory is deferential to tradition. Cobban
also believes that the traditional mode, in which a sense of history is instilled to the full, is the right way to consider the problems of political theory. It is true that the past acts as a valuable guide in our endeavour of theory–building and teaches us not to be too sure of our originality. It also hints that it is possible to think in ways other than those which are fashionable and dominant, besides shedding light on the sources. The historical understanding also sensitises us about the failings of the past generations and ties them with
the collective wisdom of the present and promotes imaginativeness in us.
Over and above this, the historical conception also contributes significantly to our normative vision. The history of ideas may tell us that our social and political universe is a product of things whose root lies in the past. And knowing them better would tell us how we have certain values, norms and moral expectations and from where they have come. With this sense in us, it is possible to interrogate these values and critically assess their utility. But a blind adherence to this conception is not without its folly. The novelty of the project called political theory is that each specific situation is unique, riddled with new challenges. Hence, worth of the past sometimes becomes redundant and could even be a hindrance, if one is oblivious of this aspect. Therefore, the utility of this approach in political theory beyond a certain level is doubtful as it is always wedded to outmoded ideas from outmoded ages. The suggestive values of the ideas remain, but the theoretical function recedes considerably.

Normative Approach

The normative conception in political theory is known by different names. Some people prefer to call it philosophical theory, while others refer to it as ethical theory. The normative conception is based on the belief that the world and its events can be interpreted in terms of logic, purpose and ends with the help of the theorist's intuition, reasoning, insights and experiences.

In other words, it is a project of philosophical speculation about values. The questions which are asked by the normativists would be: what should be the end of political institutions? What should inform the relationship between the individual and other social organisations? What arrangements in society can become model or ideal and what rules and principles should govern it? One may say that their concerns are moral and the purpose is to build an ideal

type.
Hence, it is these theorists who have always conceived 'utopia' in the realm of political ideas through their powerful imagination. Normative political theory leans heavily towards political philosophy, because it derives its knowledge of the good life from it and also uses it as a framework in its endeavour to create
absolute norms. In fact, their tools of theorisation are borrowed from political philosophy and therefore, they always seek to established inter-relationships among concepts and look for coherence in the phenomena as well as in their theories, which are typical examples of a philosophical outlook. Leo Strauss
has strongly advocated the case for normative theory and has argued that political things by nature are subject to approval or disapproval and it is difficult to judge them in any other terms, except as good or bad and justice or injustice. But the problem with the normativists is that while professing values which they cherish, they portray them as universal and absolute. They do not realise that their urge to create absolute standard for goodness is not without pitfalls. Ethical values are relative to time and space with a heavy subjective content in them, which precludes the possibility of any creation of absolute standard. We will do well to remember that even a political theorist is a subjective instrument in the assessment of the world and these insights are conditioned by many factors, which may be ideological in nature. The
exponents of empirical theory criticise normativism for:

a) Relativity of values
b) Cultural basis of ethics and norms
c) Ideological content in the enterprise and
d) Abstract and utopian nature of the project.

But in the distant past those who championed normative theory always tried to connect their principles with the understanding of the reality of their times. In recent times, again the old sensibility within the normative theory has re-emerged and the passion for good life and good society has been matched by
methodological and empirical astuteness. John Rawls' A Theory of Justice is a case in point which attempts to anchor logical and moral political theory in empirical findings. Rawls, with his imagination, creates 'original position' to connect normative philosophical arguments with real world concerns about distributive justice and the welfare state.

Empirical Approach

What has dominated political theory in the twentieth century is not normativism, but another conception known as empirical political theory which derives theories from empirical observations. Empirical political theory refuses to accord the status of knowledge to those theories which indulge in value judgements. Naturally, therefore, normative political theory is debunked as a mere statement of opinion and preferences. The drive for value – free theory started in order to make the field of political theory scientific and objective and hence a more reliable guide for action. This new orientation came to be known as positivism. Under the spell of positivism, political theorists set out to attain scientific knowledge about political phenomena based on the principle which could be empirically verified and proved. Thus, they attempted to create a natural science of society and in this endeavour; philosophy was made a mere adjunct of science. Such an account of theory also portrayed the role of a theorist as of a disinterested observer, purged of all commitments and drained of all values.

This empirical project in political theory was premised on the empiricist theory of knowledge which claims to have the full blown criteria to test what constitutes truth and falsehood. The essence of this criterion is lodged in the experimentation and the verification principle. When political theory was reeling under this influence, a so called revolution started and became popular as the 'Behavioural Revolution'. This revolution reached a commanding position within political theory in the 1950's and engulfed the entire field of study and research by advocating new features. They included:

a) Encouragement to quantitative technique in analysis
b) Demolition of the normative framework and promotion of empirical research which can be susceptible to statistical tests

c) Non – acceptance and rejection of the history of ideas
d) Focus on micro–study as it was more amenable to empirical treatment
e) Glorification of specialisation
f) Procurement of data from the behaviour of the individual and
g) Urge for value – free research.

In fact, the behavioural climate got surcharged by an anti – theory mood and those who lambasted theory in a conventional sense had a field day. Theory was caricatured and made synonymous with ideology, abstraction, metaphysics and utopia. Some adventurists even advocated farewell to theory as an enterprise. In the zeal of attaining objective knowledge, they even reduced thought to an aspect of reality and blurred the distinction between thought and reality. Thus, they soon attracted the ire and fire of some philosophers of science who offered a vision for a post – positivist approach to science. Karl Popper set the new mood by laying down the principle of 'falsification' as a criterion of scientific knowledge and argued that all knowledge was conjectural, tentative and far from the final truth. The real turn or breakthrough came in the philosophy of science when Thomas Kuhn, Imre Lakatos and Mary Hesse blasted the so called scientific theory. Kuhn's book "The Structure of Scientific Revolution" was a pioneer in bringing out the shortcomings and failures of the positivist theory and it demonstrated how all cognitions were dependent on understanding and interpretation as a means of inter-subjective communication. Kuhn cogently argued that it was not only the irrational conventions which lurked behind the construction of the semantic framework, but were also informed by rational discourses framed by interpretation and criticism.

CHAPTER V

Ceitical and Contemporary Perspectives in Political Theory

Feminist Approach

The feminist approach to the study of politics is a new age development in the evolution of Political Science. The approach emerged with growing awareness of the rights of women. Feminism refers to abroad range of ideas, approaches and ideologies directed towards advocating for gender and sex equality for women. Feminism is a movement that seeks to achieve equality and social rights for women in all key areas which includes education, personal, economic, employment and cultural sphere of human endeavors. Activists of the feminist movements have used social and political theories to campaign for women's rights and freedom where sexuality and gender-based political thinking have created imbalances for the womenfolk in the society.

The feminist movements have also campaigned for the protection of the girl child and women from sexual harassment, rape and violence within the home. The campaigns and the activities of feminist activists over several centuries have greatly improved the lots of women in several areas and in several societies. Feminist activists have successfully used campaigns for the rights of women to secure a broad range of opportunities such as the right to vote and be voted for, the right to own property, the rights to equal pay or fair wages, the right to hold public office, the right to enter legal contracts and the right to have maternity leave and equal rights within marriage. Though feminist movements have achieved a lot for the womenfolk yet some categories of feminism continued to be criticized for being ethnic and class-specific.

Evolution of Feminism

Feminism as a political force and movement can be divided in three waves:-

1. Women's suffrage movements of the 19th and early 20th century.
2. Second wave began in the 1960s. It was concerned with legal and social equality of women i.e. ending the legal sex discrimination. Right for women to have access and equal opportunity to the workplace.
3. Third waves the continuation of second wave in 1990s. Concerned about the question of sexuality and reproductive rights.

Different Kinds of Feminism

Liberal Feminism:

This kind of feminism works within the structure of mainstream society to integrate women into it and make it more responsive to individual women's rights, but does not directly challenge the system itself or the ideology behind women's oppression. The suffragist movement is an example.

Radical Feminism:

Radical feminism views patriarchy and sexism as the most elemental factor in women's oppression-cutting across all others from race and age to culture, caste and class. It questions the very system and ideology behind women's subjugation. The term often refers to the women's movements emerging from the civil rights, peace and other liberation movements at a time when people increasingly were questioning different forms of oppression and power. Radical feminists, seeking to understand the roots of women's subordination, have provided the major theoretical understanding that has served as the basis for the inspiration and analysis guiding women's movements around the world.

Black Feminism:

School of thought which argues that sexism, class oppression, gender identity and racism are inextricably bound together the way these concepts relate to each other is called intersectionality. The term intersectionality theory was first coined by legal scholar Kimberle Crenshaw in 1989. In her work, Crenshaw discussed Black Feminism, which argues that the experience of being a black woman cannot be understood in terms of being black or of being a woman. Each concept is considered independently, but must include the interactions, which frequently reinforce each other. The Combahee River Collective argued in 1974 that the liberation of black women entails freedom for all people, since it would require the end of racism, sexism and class oppression.

Marxist and Socialist Feminism:

Feminists, grounded in Marxist and socialist analysis, attribute women's oppression principally to the capitalist economic system where global corporate power prevails. Many other feminists believe that this form of power seen in the class system is a crucial factor in women's subordination but see patriarchy as the major force behind women's subjugation.

Cultural Feminism:

Cultural Feminism emphasizes essential differences between men and women in terms of biology, personality and behavior. Women are seen to have different and superior virtues that provide the foundation for a shared identity, solidarity and sisterhood. Since by nature women are viewed as kinder and gentler than men, it follows that if women were in power, the world would be a better place. In the 1960s and 70s, some women supported the idea of forming separate women-only cultures.

Eco-Feminism:

This form of feminism views patriarchy and its focus on control and domination not only as a source of women's oppression but as being harmful to humanity as well as destructive of all living creatures and the earth itself. Combining a more comprehensive analysis of power often with a greater spiritual vision, eco-feminists see women's rights and empowerment linked to political, economic, social and cultural factors that benefit all living creatures and Mother Nature herself.

Supporters of Feminism

Mary Wollstonecraft: Wollstonecraft's A Vindication of the Rights of Women (1792) is usually regarded as the first text of modem feminism and was written against the backdrop of the French Revolution, many years before the emergence of the women's suffrage movement. In arguing that women should be entitled to the same rights and privileges as men on the grounds that they are human beings, she established what was to become the core principle of liberal feminism.

Simone de Beauvoir (1906-86): A French novelist, playwright and social critic, Beauvoir helped to reopen the issue of gender politics and foreshadowed some of the themes later developed in radical feminism. She highlighted the extent to which the masculine is represented as the positive or the norm, while the feminine is portrayed as 'other'. Such 'otherness' fundamentally limits women's freedom and prevents them from expressing their full humanity. Beauvoir placed her faith in rationality and critical analysis as the means of exposing this process and giving women responsibility for their own lives. Her key feminist work is The Second Sex (1949).

Kate Millett (1934-) A US writer and sculptor, Millett developed radical feminism into a systematic theory that clearly stood apart from established liberal and socialist traditions. She portrays patriarchy as a 'social constant' running through all political, social and economic structures and grounded in a process of conditioning that operates largely through the family, 'patriarchy's chief institution'. She supports consciousness-raising as a means of challenging patriarchal oppression and has advocated the abolition and replacement of the conventional family. Millett's major work is Sexual Politics (1970).

Juliet Mitchell (1940-) A New Zealand-born British writer, Mitchell is one of the most influential theorists of socialist feminism. She has adopted a modern Marxist perspective that allows for the interplay of economic, social, political and cultural forces in society and has warned that since patriarchy has cultural and ideological roots, it cannot be overthrown simply by replacing capitalism with socialism. Mitchell was also one of the first feminists to use psychoanalytical theory as a means of explaining sexual difference. Her major works included Women's Estate (1971), Psychoanalysis and Feminism (1974) and Feminine Sexuality (1985).

Shulamith Firestone (1945-) A Canadian author and political activist, Firestone developed a theory of radical feminism that adapted Marxism to the analysis to the role of women. She argues that sexual differences stem not from conditioning but from a 'natural division of labour' within the 'biological family'. Society is thus structured not through the process of production, but through the process of reproduction. Women can, then, achieve emancipation only if they transcend their biological natures and escape from the 'curse of Eve' by the use of modern technology such as test-tube babies and artificial wombs. Firestone's best known work is The Dialectic of Sex (1970).

Catherine A. MacKinnon (1946-) A US academic and political activist, Mackinnon has made a major contribution to feminist legal theory. In her view, law in an liberal state is one of the principal devices through which women's silence and subordination is maintained. In the absence of gender equality, the 'normal' status of women is inevitably defined through the application of male values and practices. She has also argued that female oppression is based in sexuality and that pornography is the root cause of that oppression. MacKinnon's major works include Sexual Harassment and Working Women (1979), Towards a Feminist Theory of the State (1989) and Only Words (1993).

Features of the Feminist Approach

Evolution of feminism and the growth of different schools of thought on feminism views political theory from the female perspective. The main features of the feminist approach are as follows:

1] Stands for women's liberation and empowerment of women:

Feminism is a belief in the right of women and equality with men. It takes the view for the betterment and emancipation of women in society, supported for women's rights in politics and in life.

2] Root of all problems is gender inequality:

Feminist thinkers emphasise that gender inequality to be the root cause of all ills in the state. It condemn the established theories of the state on the ground that such ignore the equal rights of women and subjugate them to male dominance in all areas e.g. all governments are dominated by men, all decisions that are taken at the local, national and international level are made from the male perspective. Feminists have highlighted what they see as the political relationship between the sexes the supremacy of man and the subjection of women.

3] Criticizes Male Bias:

The feminist approach to Political Studies is based on the assumption that the government it laws, its members, the bureaucracy and civil society all are patriarchal. They are based on a system wherein men are considered to be superior to women. The feminist theory criticizes this male bias and holds it to be unjust.

4] Tackles Problems of Women:

The feminist approach formulates theories that seek to resolve gender bias. It finds solutions to the problems of women and suggests methods by which the government can empower women.

5] Clubbed with other approaches:

The feminist approach is usually adopted in conjunction with another approach such as the normative, empirical, comparative, sociological approaches e.g. a study on the voting behavior of women would adopt a feminist empirical approach.

Evaluation of the Feminist approach:

Critics of the approach claim that feminist theories have the following drawbacks:

1] Critics say that the assumption of the feminist approach that it is only men who create a woman unfriendly world is incorrect. Many times women are woman's worst enemy e.g. In India mother in law and daughter in law relationship.

2] Critics say that tracing all women's problems to gender bias is a wrong way to approach issues. Some issues are common to both genders.

Importance

a] It is concerned about the problems of women. If not for feminists, perhaps women's empowerment would not have been as great a success at it is. Feminist political research studies and finds solutions to problems of women e.g. problems such as poverty among women, crime against women, female foeticides, etc.

b] The feminist approach adds a woman's touch to global leadership. Peace initiatives, cultural exchanges, literacy drives and medical aid to needy.

c] Feminism has gained growing respectability as a distinctive school of political thought. It has shed new light upon established concepts such as power, domination and equality but also introduced a new sensitivity and language into politics.

d] The domestic, professional and public roles of women, at least in developed societies have undergone a major transformation due to feminist approach and women's movement.

Postmodernism

Postmodernism is a controversial and confusing term that was first used to describe experimental movements in western architecture and cultural development in general. Postmodern thought originated principally in continental Europe, especially France and constitutes a challenge to the type of academic political theory that has come to be the norm in the Anglo-American world. Since the 1970s, however, postmodern and post structural political theories have become increasingly fashionable. Their basis lies in a perceived social shift-from modernity to post modernity- and a related cultural and intellectual shift-from modernism to postmodernism. Modern societies were seen to be structured by industrialization and class solidarity, social identity being largely determined by one's position within the productive system. Postmodern societies, on the other hand are increasingly fragmented and pluralistic 'information' societies in which individuals are transformed from producers to consumers and individualism replaces class, religious and ethnic loyalties. Postmodernity is thus linked to postindustrialism, the development of a society no longer dependent upon manufacturing industry, but more reliant upon knowledge and communication.

Postmodernist thought has been criticized from two angles. In the first place, it has been accused of relativism in that it holds that different modes of knowing are equally valid and thus rejects the idea that even science is able reliably to distinguish between truth and falsehood. Secondly, it has been charged with conservatism on the grounds that a non- foundationalist political stance offers no perspective from which the existing order may be criticized and no basis for the construction of an alternative social order. Nevertheless the attraction of postmodern theory is its remorseless questioning of apparently solid realities and accepted beliefs. Its general emphasis upon discourse, debate and democracy reflects the fact that to reject hierarchies of ideas is also to reject any political and social hierarchies.

Principles

The following principles appear elemental to postmodernists:

1. Rejection of the ultimate faith on science:

Modernism was established on the belief in science and rationality. The destruction and trauma of the two world wars had formed a negative attitude towards science and technology in modem mind. Postmodernists have observed that scientific developments led to industrialization causing damages to humankind in the form of poverty, unemployment, environmental pollution, etc.

2. There is no absolute truth:

Postmodernists believe that the notion of truth is a contrived illusion misused by people and special interest groups to gain power over others. Truth and error are synonymous - facts, postmodernists claim are too limiting to determine anything. Changing erratically, what is fact today can be false tomorrow.

3. Self-conceptualization and rationalization:

Traditional logic and objectivity are spurned by postmodernists. Preferring to rely on opinions rather than embrace facts, postmodernists spurn the scientific method.

4. Traditional authority is false and corrupt:

Postmodernists speak out against the constraints of religious morals and secular authority. They wage intellectual revolution to voice their concerns about traditional.

5. Disillusionment with modernism:

Postmodernists rue the unfulfilled promises of science, technology, government and religion.

6. Morality is personal:

Believing ethics to be relative, postmodernists subject morality to personal opinion. They define morality as each person's private code of ethics without the need to follow traditional values and rules.

7. Globalization:

Many postmodernists claim that national boundaries are a hindrance to human communication. Nationalism, they believe, causes wars. Therefore, postmodernists often propose internationalism and uniting separate countries.

8. Rejected the Idea of Representation:

Postmodernism rejects all representation operations in any form of representation. In the sense that there is a group of individuals representing the rest of the people in parliament. The fundamental problem is the lack of understanding and inability to represent the other, because of the differences in the political discourse of each party and the different meanings of terns between cultures and even among members of the same culture, hampering the process of representation.

Supporter of Postmodernism

Friedrich Nietzsche: A German philosopher, Nietzsche is invariably regarded as the most important precursor of postmodernism. His work stresses the importance of will, especially the 'will to power' and emphasizes that people create their own world and make their own values. This is most memorably expressed in the assertion that 'God is dead'. Nietzsche's nihilism, the rejection of all moral and political principles encouraged later postmodern theorists to regard truth as a fiction and to link beliefs and values to the assertion of power.

Martin Heidegger (1889-1976): A German philosopher, Heidegger also a precursor of postmodernism had a considerable impact upon the development of phenomenology and existentialism. Fundamental to his philosophical system was the question of the meaning of being, by which he meant self-conscious existence. All previous political philosophies had made the mistake of starting out from a conception of human nature rather than recognizing the human essence as a 'realm of disclosure'. This had led to the dominance of technology over human existence, from which, Heidegger believed, humans could escape by developing a more receptive relationship to being. Heidegger's most famous work is Being and Time (1927).

Jean-Francois Lyotard (1924-) A French philosopher, Lyotard was primarily responsible for popularizing the term postmodern and for giving it its most succinct definition: 'An incredulity towards metanarratives.' By this, he meant a scepticism about all creeds and ideologies that are based upon universal theories of history which view society as a coherent totality. This stems from science's loss of authority as it has fragmented into a number of forms of discourse and as 'performativity' or efficiency has displaced truth as its standard of value. Lyotard's post-Marxism also reflects his belief that communism has been eliminated as an alternative to liberal capitalism. His most important work is The Postmodern Condition (1979).

Michel Foucault: A French philosopher, Foucault was primarily concerned with forms of knowledge and the construction of the human subject. His early work analysed different branches of knowledge as 'archaeologies leading to an emphasis upon discourse' or 'discursive formation'. Central to this was his belief that knowledge is deeply enmeshed in power, truth always being a social construct and that power can be productive as well as prohibitive.

Jacques Derrida (1930-) A French philosopher, Derrida is the main proponent of deconstruction, although it is a term he is reluctant to use. Deconstruction (sometimes used interchangeably with poststructuralism) is the task of missing questions about the 'texts' that constitute cultural life, exposing complications and contradictions of which their 'authors' are not fully conscious and for which they are not fully responsible. Derrida's concept of 'difference' rejects the idea that there are fixed differences in language and allows for a constant sliding between meanings in that there are no polar opposites.

Richard Rorty (1931-) A US philosopher, Rorty has focused increasingly upon political issues having established his reputation in the analysis of language and mind. His early work rejected the idea that there is an objective, transcendental standpoint from which beliefs can be judged, leading to the conclusion that philosophy itself should be understood as nothing more than a conversation. Nevertheless, he supports a pragmatic brand of liberalism that overlaps at times with social democracy for which reason he has reservations about some of the relativist trends in postmodernism. Rorty's best-known works include Philosophy and the Mirror of Nature (1979), Consequences of Pragmatism (1982) and Contingency, Irony and Solidarity (1989). Include Writing and Difference (1967), Margins of Philosophy (1972) and Spectres of Marx.

CHAPTER VI

Political Theory and Practice

Theoretical Politics

1. It provides theoretical knowledge of different aspects of state.
2. It gives theoretical education about government and administration.
3. It provides theoretical meaning of lawmaking.
4. It assumes that the state is made by individuals and discusses relations between the state and individuals as well as international law.

Applied Politics

1. It gives a good idea about the state-formation.
2. It gives real knowledge about the administration and functions of government.
3. It discusses law making and powers of judiciary.
4. It describes the real relations among states.

Practical Politics: Definition And Examples

Human life in society has an important role in the political method of a country. Humans, in their position as social beings, will always interact with other humans in an effort to create their necessities of life.

The basic needs of human life are insufficient, such as eating, drinking, biology, clothes and shelter (house). More than that, it also includes the need for self-recognition and respect from others in the form of pride, payment of work, status as a member of society, a member of a certain political party and so on.

Every citizen, in his daily life is almost always in contact with practical political aspects, whether symbolic or not. In the implementation of the process, it can occur immediately or indirectly with political practices.

Practical Politics: Definition

The meaning of practical politics is a world where all intentions, motives, interests and determination are present side by side and co-exist with each other to fight for power. In plain view, the power referred to is none other than a position, position or position. But implicitly, what is fought over is the authority and authority to make public decisions.

In the past, when the concept of democracy was not yet as conceptual as it is today, politics was practically nothing but a "war or physical clash" between two or more camps that destroyed each other to gain power.

However, when the concept of political democracy has been grounded as it is today, practical politics has resembled a contestation of mutually assassinating characters, destroying each other's strategies and tactics, attacking each other's territorial bases and competing with each other to receive public sympathy.

Practical Political Examples

- What was carried out by the PKI and PNI in destroying HMI to form a power association.
- Political parties that use many celebrities where they are public figures who have been famous to attract the hearts and support of the community.
- During the New Order era, the TNI became a political tool which should be neutral for all groups.

- Carrying out political party campaigns on campus where the campus should be in a neutral zone and not taking sides with any group in a political context.
- Timses for people's leadership candidates who distributed basic food and money (money policy) to gain popular support.
- Making political friends as sacrifices to cover up the bigger corruption within parties and government institutions.

CHAPTER VII

The Grammar of Democracy

A democracy without a dissenter in it is impossible to imagine. In the exercise of free thought, free men are sure to express free speech. So, even if such thought is revolting or its manner of expression is despicable, a mature democracy will tolerate it and encourage its publication.

Dissenting is very much a part of history of human civilization. Dissent can't be defined as anti-national. Going back to 1570, Martin Luther nailed on the door of a church in Germany, 95 objections to the Catholic faith which led to the evolution of Protestanism. Galileo challenged the Church through his statement of the fact that the Earth and other planets revolve round the Sun.

Progress of mankind is all about a history of informed dissent. History has survived innumerable dissenting voices and all sorts of high quality creative activities in various areas of human venture are nothing but dissent.

In the age that we live, democracy is favoured as the most acceptable form of governance. What makes democracy different from the colonial regime, Hitler's Germany or Stalin's USSR is the right to dissent that democracy bestows upon its citizen. While dissent could lead to the severest of punishments or even loss of life in colonial India or under Hitler's and Stalin's rule, dissent in democracy is an exercise of one's right without the fear of victimization as long as it doesn't lead to inhuman or unconstitutional action.

Dissent can be treated as salt of democracy. Tagging the dissenters as anti-nationals has diluted the whole idea and basis of democracy and its fundamentals.

The house arrest of five activists by the Pune Police who were allegedly suspected to be involved in the violence in Bhima-Koregaon in Mahrashtra and the questions put forth by the police on their belief system just because their house interiors had photos of Phule and Ambedkar presents a harsh reality of the modern society that we dwell in. In the same case, the Supreme Court had stated that "Dissent is the safety valve of democracy. If dissent is not allowed, the pressure cooker will burst. Compress the pressure cooker."

In debating for nationalism and patriotism, we tend to forget that dissent is a legitimate political expression that stands as valid in a democracy. If a certain path is chosen by the society, then dissent lends an alternative route in case the one chosen by the society turns out to be wrong or dangerous.

Dissidents, who question the system argue with the administration and put forth their views before the government is often labeled as "urban naxals" and their voices are termed as "seditious." This tactic works only for diverting the attention of the masses from the issues of much essential economic management and social development. The real core issues that are for the betterment of society are put on a stand-by mode and the media and political establishment put across interrogations and humiliating remarks on those who raise their voices. Everyone just stops caring about the real venomous parasites – corruption, mismanagement, unemployment and inflation - which are the real issues. Efforts are made to suppress such voices which are really a matter for the improvement and betterment of the country.

The murders of writers Dabholkar, Kalburgi and Gauri Lankesh Gauri Lankesh is proof bigotry and intolerance have put a fatal tear in our national soul. Even actors like Amir Khan and Nasiruddin when spoke their minds publicly are termed as anti-nationals and are trolled on social media with hateful words, challenging their right to free speech.

Even students are not spared from being tagged as seditious when they raise their voices against something irrational. However, thanks to the non-governmental organizations which lend a platform to civil society to dissent in an informed and reasoned manner. Not just this, they also provides a mechanism for the ruled to keep a check on the rulers. Though not all NGOs act clean and legitimate on their part, yet there are few that operate transparently and judiciously and it is the power of such NGOs that wield support to the increased demand for real and operational democracy. Be it the Right to Information Act or the Protection of Plant Varieties and Farmers' Rights Act, it has been through the support of such voices that the country is having some relief.

How can we ignore the fact that it has been the ability of India to express without fear which has brought joy to its friends and amazement to its adversaries? Nor can we forget the proclamation of Zulfikar Ali Bhutto that he made from his death-row cell in Pakistan that “India is more heterogeneous than Pakistan, but India has been kept in one piece by the noise and chaos of her democracy,” in spite of his earlier advocacy of a thousand-year war with India.

The dissents expressed at crucial times in the history of this nation have given it the base of growth. The Nandas of Magadh were complacent in the face of Alexander’s invasions and faced the dissent of Kautilya, who later created the Mauryan Empire. The orthodoxy of his times was dissented by Budhha and then came to revelation the “Eightfold Path”. The fading of Sanatana Dharma was questioned by Adi Shankara which led to its resurrection. Further, the dissent of the soldiers at Barrackpore and Meerut led to the First War of Independence in 1857.

Those who gave us our path to an independent India were none other than a long line of dissenters, from Lokmanya Tilak to Bose, Nehru and Gandhi. Even the Indian Constitution, which has been endured through all these years has been given to us by a man who dissented from even Mahatma Gandhi.

While we revel in the wisdom of the morrow, we must accept the fact that it was the call for total revolution by Jayapraksah Narayan, which led to the imposition of Emergency and also the consensus against the dictatorship.

The fact that the right to life was inherent in humans and not a gift of the Constitution should be reminded to us time and again. It is also a point of great significance in the current context when speaking one’s mind on some issue is put across the test of fire. It should be a notion made clear in our mindsets that this right to life and dissent can’t be suspended.

Rather than keeping one’s thought as unexpressed, it’s ideal to be voiced and rejected in the pool of ideas, no matter how imperfect it is. If all such ideas and voices would have been kept within and never have been expressed, how would we have so proudly called ourselves the citizens of world’s largest and most flourishing democracy!

And for that matter, what is the true idea of democracy, isn’t it the free men who willingly commit to the needs of citizenship of a free country.

Who suppresses dissents and dissidents, is not one who supports and believes in democracy but rather hails from totalitarian regime.

What is Democracy?

Democracy means rule by the people. The name is employed for various sorts of government, where the people can participate within the decisions that affect the way their community is run. A democratic government is a system of government that is elected by the whole adult population, people over the age of 18 years. They do this by choosing someone to represent their community at an area, state and federal level. The purpose of the elected government is to protect the people and promote their rights, interests and welfare to the benefit of everyone.

Where the term democracy derives from?

The word democracy originated in ancient Greece over 2400 years ago.

‘Demos’ means common people and ‘Kratos’ means strength.

Democracy as we know it today as freedom system of government in which citizens exercise power directly or elect representatives from amongst themselves. The term democracy first appeared in ancient Greek political and philosophical Fort in the city state of Athens during classical antiquity even the word democracy comes from the agent Greek language demos meaning people and kratos meaning strength. Athenians established what is generally held is the first democracy in 580 - 507 BC.

Cleisthenes is known as the father of Athenian democracy. Athenian democracy took the form of a direct democracy and it had to distinguishing features the random selection of ordinary citizens to fill the few existing government, administrative and judicial officers and the legislative assembly consisting of all the senior citizens. All eligible citizens were allowed to speak and vote in the assembly, which set the laws of the city state. However opinion citizenship excluded women slaves and foreigners, so wasn't that free of world in voters we know today, but it was a good start.

The Roman Republic contributed significantly to many aspects of democracy only a minority of Romans for citizens with votes in elections for representatives additionally the Roman model of governments inspired many political thinkers, health centuries and days modern representative democracies imitate more the Roman, the Greek models because it was a state in which supreme power was held by the people and their elected representatives and which had an elected or nominated leader. Another example that the natives in North America which between around 1450-1680 AD also develop the form of democratic society before they came in contact with the Europeans. This indicates the forms of democracy may have been invented in other societies around the world. In medieval times, most regions in Europe or ruled by clergy or future loads, almost no democracy remain from the ancient Greeks or Romans in the parliament.

The first English parliament was created in 1265 starting separation of powers in state many laws and rules are made after this event in the whole of Europe. The power of kings began to fade to local nobles and afterwards to the people after some centuries the case of proclamations in 1610 in England decided that the king by his proclamation or other ways cannot change any part of the common law or statute law all the customs of the realm awesome after World War One. Austria-Hungary and the Ottoman Empire collapse giving the opportunity to oppressed nations to be free in 1918, the United Kingdom granted the right to vote to women and in 1928 granted women and men equal rights. In 1920 women stop the right to vote in the United States and in 1944 in France. In 1920, the US for granted full US citizenship to Americas indigenous peoples.

History of direct Democracy

One strand of thought sees direct democracy as common and widespread in pre-state societies. The earliest well-documented direct democracy is claimed to be the Athenian democracy of the 5th century BC. The main bodies within the Athenian democracy were the assembly, composed of male citizens; the boul, composed of 500 citizens; and therefore the law courts, composed of a huge number of jurors chosen by lot, with no judges. Ancient Attica had only about 30,000 male citizens, but several thousand of them were politically active in each year and many of them quite regularly for years on end. The Athenian democracy was direct not only within the sense that the assembled people made decisions, but also within the sense that the people - through the assembly, boul, and law courts - controlled the whole political process, and an outsized proportion of citizens were involved constantly in publicly affairs. Most modern democracies, being representative, not direct, don't resemble the Athenian system.

Also relevant to the history of direct democracy is that the history of Ancient Rome, specifically during the Roman Republic, traditionally founded around 509 BC. Rome displayed many aspects of democracy, both direct and indirect, from the age of Roman monarchy all the thanks to the collapse of the Roman Empire.

While the Roman senate was the most body with historical longevity, lasting from the Roman kingdom until after the collapse of the Western Roman Empire in 476 AD, it did not embody a purely democratic approach, being made up - during the late republic - of former elected officials, providing advice instead of creating law.

The democratic aspect of the constitution resided within the Roman popular assemblies, where the people organised into centuriae or into tribes - counting on the assembly - and cast votes on various matters, including elections and laws, proposed before them by their elected magistrates. Some classicists have argued that the Roman Republic deserves the label of democracy, with universal suffrage for man citizens, popular sovereignty and transparent deliberation of public affairs. Many historians mark the top of the Republic with the lex Titia, passed on 27 November 43 BC, which eliminated many oversight provisions.

Ultramodern Direct Republic also occurs within the Crow Nation, a Native American Tribe in the United States of America. The lineage is organized around a General Council formed of all voting-age members. The General Council has the power to produce fairly - binding opinions through blackballs. The General Council was first elevated in the 1948 Crow Constitution and was upheld and re-instated with the 2002 Constitution.

Some of the issues girding the affiliated notion of a direct republic using the Internet and other dispatches technologies are dealt with in the composition one-democracy and below under the heading Electronic direct republic. Further compactly, the conception of open-source governance applies principles of the free software movement to the governance of people, allowing the entire crowd to share in government directly, as much or as little as they please.

Direct republic is the base of challenger and left-libertarian political study. Direct republic has been supported by challenger thinkers since its commencement, and direct republic as a political proposition has been largely told by anarchism.

A democracy is a form of government that empowers the people to exercise political control, limits the power of the head of state, provides for the separation of powers between governmental entities and ensures the protection of natural rights and civil liberties. In practice, democracy takes many different forms. Along with the two most common types of democracies—direct and representative—variants such as participatory, liberal, parliamentary, pluralist, constitutional and socialist democracies can be found in use today.

Key Takeaways: Democracy

Democracy, literally meaning "rule by the people," empowers individuals to exercise political control over the form and functions of their government.

While democracies come in several forms, they all feature competitive elections, freedom of expression and protection of individual civil liberties and human rights.

In most democracies, the needs and wishes of the people are represented by elected lawmakers who are charged with writing and voting on laws and setting policy.

When creating laws and policies, the elected representatives in a democracy strive to balance conflicting demands and obligations to maximize freedom and protect individual rights.

Despite the prominence in the headlines of non-democratic, authoritarian states like China, Russia, North Korea, and Iran, democracy remains the world's most commonly practiced form of government. In 2018, for example, a total of 96 out of 167 countries (57%) with populations of at least 500,000 were democracies of some type. Statics show that the percentage of democracies among the world's governments has been increasing since the mid-1970s, currently standing just short of its post-World War II high of 58% in 2016.

A democracy is a form of government that empowers the people to exercise political control, limits the power of the head of state, provides for the separation of powers between governmental entities, and ensures the protection of natural rights and civil liberties. In practice, democracy takes many different forms. Along with the two most common types of democracies—direct and representative—variants such as participatory, liberal, parliamentary, pluralist, constitutional, and socialist democracies can be found in use today.

Democratic Principles

While their opinions vary, a consensus of political scientists agree that most democracies are based on six foundational elements:

(i) Popular sovereignty: The principle that the government is created and maintained by the consent of the people through their elected representatives.

(ii) An Electoral System: Since according to the principle of popular sovereignty, the people are the source of all political power, a clearly defined system of conducting free and fair elections is essential.

(iii) Public Participation: Democracies rarely survive without the active participation of the people. Health democracies enable and encourage the people to take part in their political and civic processes.

(iv) Separation of Powers: Based on a suspicion of power concentrated in a single individual—like a king—or group, the constitutions of most democracies provide that political powers be separated and shared among the various governmental entities.

(v) Human Rights: Along with their constitutionally enumerated rights freedoms, democracies protect the human rights of all citizens. In this context, human rights are those rights considered inherent to all human beings, regardless of nationality, sex, national or ethnic origin, color, religion, language, or any other considerations.

(vi) A Rule of Law: Also called due process of law, the rule of law is the principle that all citizens are accountable to laws that are publicly created and equitably enforced in a manner consistent with human rights by an independent judicial system.

Democracy Definition

According to Abraham Lincoln, "Democracy is a government of the people, by the people, and for the people."

Meaning “rule by the people,” democracy is a system of government that not only allows but requires the participation of the people in the political process to function properly. U.S. President Abraham Lincoln, in his famed 1863 Gettysburg Address may have best-defined democracy as a “...government of the people, by the people, for the people...”

Semantically, the term democracy comes from the Greek words for “people” (dēmos) and “rule” (karatos). However, achieving and preserving a government by the people—a “popular” government—is far more complicated than the concept’s semantic simplicity might imply. In creating the legal framework under which the democracy will function, typically a constitution, several crucial political and practical questions must be answered.

Is “rule by the people” even appropriate for the given state? Do the inherent freedoms of a democracy justify dealing with its complex bureaucracy and electoral processes, or would the streamlined predictability of a monarchy, for example, be preferable?

Assuming a preference for democracy, which residents of the country, state, or town should enjoy the political status of full citizenship? Simply stated, who are the “people” in the “government by the people” equation? In the United States, for example, the constitutionally established doctrine of birthright citizenship provides that any person born on U.S. soil automatically becomes a U.S. citizen. Other democracies are more restrictive in bestowing full citizenship.

Which people within the democracy should be empowered to participate in it? Assuming that only adults are allowed to fully participate in the political process, should all adults be included? For example, until the enactment of the 19th Amendment in 1920, women in the United States were not allowed to vote in national elections. A democracy that excludes too many of the governed from taking part in what is supposed to be their government runs the risk of becoming an aristocracy—government by a small, privileged ruling class—or an oligarchy—government by an elite, typically wealthy, few.

If, as one of the foundational principles of democracy holds, the majority rules, what will a "proper" majority be? A majority of all citizens or a majority of citizens who vote only? When issues, as they inevitably will, divide the people, should the wishes of the majority always prevail, or should, as in the case of the American Civil Rights Movement, minorities be empowered to overcome majority rule? Most importantly, what legal or legislative mechanisms should be created to prevent the democracy from becoming a victim of what one of America's Founding Fathers, James Madison, called "the tyranny of the majority?"

Finally, how likely is it that a majority of the people will continue to believe that democracy is the best form of government for them? For a democracy to survive it must retain the substantial support of both the people and the leaders they choose. History has shown that democracy is a particularly fragile institution. In fact, of the 120 new democracies that have emerged around the world since 1960, nearly half have resulted in failed states or have been replaced by other, typically more authoritarian forms of government. It is therefore essential that democracies be designed to respond quickly and appropriately to the internal and external factors that will inevitably threaten them.

According to Dicey, "Democracy is a form of government in which the governing body is a comparatively large fraction of the entire nation".

According to Seeley: - "Democracy is a government in which every one has a share."

In the Dictionary Definition, "Democracy is a government by the people in which the supreme power is vested in the people and exercised directly by them or by their elected agents under a free electoral system."

Types of Democracy

Throughout history, more types of democracy have been identified than there are countries in the world. According to social and political philosopher Jean-Paul Gagnon, more than 2,234 adjectives have been used to describe democracy. While many scholars refer to direct and representative as the most common of these, several other types of democracies can be found around the world today. While direct democracy is unique, most other recognized types of democracy are variants of representative democracy.

These various types of democracy are generally descriptive of the particular values emphasized by the representative democracies that employ them.

Direct Democracy

Originated in Ancient Greece during the 5th century BCE, direct democracy, sometimes called "pure democracy," is considered the oldest non-authoritarian form of government. In a direct democracy, all laws and public policy decisions are made directly by a majority vote of the people, rather than by the votes of their elected representatives.

Functionally possible only in small states, Switzerland is the only example of a direct democracy applied on a national level today. While Switzerland is no longer a true direct democracy, any law passed by the popularly elected national parliament can be vetoed by a direct vote of the public. Citizens can also change the constitution through direct votes on amendments. In the United States, examples of direct democracy can be found in state-level recall elections and law-making ballot initiatives.

Representative

Also called indirect democracy, representative democracy is a system of government in which all eligible citizens elect officials to pass laws and formulate public policy on their behalf. These elected officials are expected to represent the needs and viewpoints of the people in deciding the best course of action for the nation, state, or other jurisdiction as a whole.

As the most commonly found type of democracy in use today, almost 60% of all countries employ some form of representative democracy including the United States, the United Kingdom, and France.

Participatory

In a participatory democracy, the people vote directly on policy while their elected representatives are responsible for implementing those policies. Participatory democracies rely on the citizens in setting the direction of the state and the operation of its political systems. While the two forms of government share similar ideals, participatory democracies tend to encourage a higher, more direct form of citizen participation than traditional representative democracies.

While there are no countries specifically classified as participatory democracies, most representative democracies employ citizen participation as a tool for social and political reform. In the United States, for example, so-called "grassroots" citizen participation causes such as the Civil Rights Movement of the 1960s have led elected officials to enact laws implementing sweeping social, legal, and political policy changes.

Liberal

Liberal democracy is loosely defined as a form of representative democracy that emphasizes the principles of classical liberalism—an ideology advocating the protection of individual civil liberties and economic freedom by limiting the power of the government. Liberal democracies employ a constitution, either statutorily codified, as in the United States or uncodified, as in the United Kingdom, to define the powers of the government, provide for a separation of those powers, and enshrine the social contract.

Liberal democracies may take the form of a constitutional republic, like the United States, or a constitutional monarchy, such as the United Kingdom, Canada, and Australia.

Parliamentary

In a parliamentary democracy, the people directly elect representatives to a legislative parliament. Similar to the U.S. Congress, the parliament directly represents the people in making necessary laws and policy decisions for the country.

In parliamentary democracies such as the United Kingdom, Canada, and Japan, the head of government is a prime minister, who is first elected to parliament by the people, then elected prime minister by a vote of the parliament. However, the prime minister remains a member of the parliament and thus plays an active role in the legislative process of creating and passing laws. Parliamentary democracies are typically a feature of a constitutional monarch, a system of government in which the head of state is a queen or king, whose power is limited by a constitution.

Pluralist

In a pluralist democracy, no single group dominates politics. Instead, organized groups within the people compete to influence public policy. In political science, the term pluralism expresses the ideology that influence should be spread among different interest groups, rather than held by a single elite group as in an aristocracy. Compared to participatory democracies, in which individuals take part in influencing political decisions, in a pluralist democracy, individuals work through groups formed around common causes hoping to win the support of elected leaders.

In this context, the pluralist democracy assumes that the government and the society as a whole benefit from a diversity of viewpoints. Examples of pluralist democracy can be seen in the impact, special interest groups, such as the National Organization for Women, have had on American politics.

Constitutional

While the exact definition continues to be debated by political scientists, constitutional democracy is generally defined as a system of government based on popular sovereignty and a rule of law in which the structures, powers, and limits of government are established by a constitution. Constitutions are intended to restrict the power of the government, typically by separating those powers between the various branches of government, as in the United States' constitution's system of federalism. In a constitutional democracy, the constitution is considered to be the "supreme law of the land."

Socialist

Democratic socialism is broadly defined as a system of government based on a socialist economy, in which most property and means of production are collectively, rather than individually, controlled by a constitutionally established political hierarchy—the government. Social democracy embraces government regulation of business and industry as a means of furthering economic growth while preventing income inequality.

While there are no purely socialist governments in the world today, elements of democratic socialism can be seen in Sweden's provision of free universal health care, education, and sweeping social welfare programs.

Necessary Conditions for the Successful Working of Democracy

The following conditions are necessary for the successful working of Democracy-

Belief in Democratic Principles- The first condition necessary for the successful working of democracy is that citizens of that country should have faith in democratic principles. They should have respect for other views and should perform their duties properly.

Economic Equality- Democracy can function smoothly in countries that do not have extremes of wealth and property. A country in which a large number of persons are poor while a few of them have plenty cannot run democratic institutions successfully.

Educated Citizens- Only educated citizens can have knowledge of their rights and duties and can exercise them properly. Uneducated citizens cannot even cast their votes properly.

High Moral Standard- Democracy can be run successfully in a country whose citizens are honest, impartial and selfless. They should not be amenable to undue pressures during elections.

Right Types of Leaders- The success of democracy depends greatly on the quality of leaders a country is able to provide. Leaders must be men of sound judgement, balanced mind, honest and of unimpeachable character.

Equal Social and Political Rights- Democracy can be successful if all the citizens are given equal social and political rights. Equality before the law, the right to vote and to fight elections should be given to all.

Sound Party System- Democracy can be successful in a country where political parties are organized on definite economic, social and political principles and not on the basis of religion or caste.

Free and Honest Press- A free press is said to be the Bible of democracy. The people should have access to free and unbiased information regarding domestic and foreign affairs.

Independent Judiciary- Independent Judiciary is also necessary for the successful working of democracy. If the judiciary is not free and independent, the right and liberties of the citizens cannot be safeguarded.

Local-Self Government- In order to make democracy successful, local institutions should be established at all levels. Local institutions (Municipalities, Panchayats etc.) serve as the training ground for democracy.

Strong Opposition- Strong and organized opposition is also necessary for the successful working of democracy. It checks the government from becoming dictatorial.

Peace and Security- Democracy can run successfully in a country where peace and security prevail. In countries that have the perpetual danger of war or revolt, democracy cannot be run successfully.

Differences between Democracy and Dictatorship

Democracy

- A democracy is a form of government in which the people possess the ultimate power.
- Democracy believes in Equality.
- It encourages free thoughts.
- People choose what is good for them.
- People can change, create and enact the laws.

Dictatorship

- Dictatorship is a form of government in which rulers possesses all the powers.
- Dictatorship believes in hierarchy.
- It suppresses free thoughts and actions.
- A dictator imposes what he/ she thinks is good for his/ her rule.
- Laws is created by the dictator with no involvement of the people.

CHAPTER VIII

Democracy: The history of an idea

Democracy is one of the oldest concept in political science. It is still relevant and much in discussion. One can safely divide today's world into (1) Democratic countries and (2) Non-democratic countries. Not only this, where there is no democracy, people are struggling to get democracy and where there is democracy, people are asking for more democracy. It shows that all over the world, democracy has become the most favoured form of government.
Democracy is a word, comprise as "demos" (people) and "kratos" (government). These are Greek words. Despite being one of the oldest concept, it is quite difficult to offer precise difination of democracy. Not only this, there are types of democracy - Liberal democracy and People's democracy. Even Hitler and Mussolini insisted that theirs is a democratic set up.

Definition of Democracy

Prof. C.D. Burns - "Democracy is a word with many meanings and some emotional colour".

The Oxford English Dictionary - "Democracy is a system of government by the whole population run usually through elected representatives".

According to Abraham Lincoln (1809-1865) - "Democracy is the government by the people, for the people and of the people."

Thus, to some, democracy 'is a form of government' to others, 'it is a way of social life'. The essence of democracy as a form of government lies in its nature of franchise, the character of electoral system and the relation between the government and the people existing in a particular nation.

Supporter of Democracy

Jean-Jacques Rousseau:

Rousseau viewed democracy as the most important means through which humans can achieve freedom or authonomy, in the sense of 'obedience to a law one prescribes to oneself'.

Joseph Schumpeter (1883-1950):

A Moravian-born US economist and sociologist Schumpeter developed an analysis of capitalism that emphasized its bureaucratics tendencies and its growing resemblance to socialism.

Crawford Brough MacPherson (1911-87):

A Canadian political theorist, Macpherson developed a leftist form of liberalism that reflects the influence of Marxism.

Robert Dahl (1915-)

A US political scientist, Dahl is a leading exponent of pluralist theory. He contrast modern Democratic with the classical democracy of Ancient Greece, using the term 'polyarchy' to refer to rule by the many, as distinct from rule by all citizens.

History of Democracy

From the anthropological studies, we came to know that democracy existed in the most primitive society that is in early parts of human civilization, when people had just started to live in group.

Growth of Democracy in West

Democracy in the ancient times in the Western soil was not so mature and effective form of government or public or social groups. In the West, there has been a gradual development of democracy from the time of Homer to its present form referred to as 'Liberal Democracy'. In Homer's time, a King needed the support of general body of freeman to make any important decisions. Also, in Athens in age of pericles a form of pure democracy prevailed where assemblies called Ecclesia played an important role in administration. In Rome, democracy came into existence after the downfall of the king and after a struggle between Patrician and plebian in which Power came in the hand of Patrician. The constitution being democratic in nature gave equal rights to the plebs to participate in the working of government. With the fall of Rome democracy, democracy in ancient times came to an end.

Many great philosopher contributed in the rise and growth of democracy in ancient Greek city-state. Thought at that time, the appearance of democracy was by no means considered as an ideal rule. Plato (428/427 B.C - 348/427 B.C) vehemently opposed democracy because, according to him we are not appropriate equipped with education 'to select the best ruler and wisest course'. He added that democracy made men excellent orators to seek votes but their selfishness ruined the state and left people helpless as their basic needs were not fulfilled with this form of government. Aristotle (384 B.C - 322 B.C) believed that democracy should be 'rule of many' that is it should not be the rule of mediocre fulfilling their vested interests but should be equally the rule of poor. He agree with his teacher's (Plato) conception of democracy that is failed to judge and select people or leaders on merits or sound education and mental level. Aristotle observed that all the forms of democracy of his time were perverted with none stable and ideal. He pointed out that merits and demerits of democracy and approved of a Mixed constitution which is a combination of asistocracy and democracy.

This idea of Mixed democracy was carried out forward by letter philosopher like Polybius, Marcus Tullius Cicero (106 B.C - 43 B.C) and Saint Augustine (345 - 430 C.E). In eighteen century democracy was again forcefully emerged with the writing of Baron De Montesquieu, Francois-Marie Arouet Voltaire (1994-1778) and Jeans Jacques Rousseau (1712-1778). With Machiavelli's 'Discourse' and Montesqiueu's 'Spirit of the law' came the dawn of modern political thought. They took democracy to be pure form of government that could be safely incorporated into State craft only as one of a mixed republicans constitution. Thomas Hobbes (1588-1679) and John Locke (1632-1704) were the early exponent of "Social Contract Theory" which sort to base political legimacy on the consent of the people.

Democracy as an Idea

Democracy as an Idea and as a political reality is fundamentally contested. Not only in the history of democracy marked by conflicting interpretation, but also and ancient and modern nation intermingle to produce ambiguous and inconsistent account of the key term of democracy. It is sometimes argued that democratic government was born in the city-state of the ancient Greece and that we inherited democratic ideals from that time. In fact however this assertion can be refuted easily. In the Greek view, we just see a democratic order would have to satisfy at least six requirements:

1. Citizen must be sufficient harmonious in their interests so that they can share and act upon a strong sense of a general good that is not in marked contradiction to their personal aims and interest.

2. Secondly they must be highly homogenous with respect to characteristics that would otherwise tend to produce political conflict and sharp disagreement over the public good.

3. The citizens body must be quite small ideally even smaller than the fourty to fifty thousand of Periclean Athens. The small size of the demos was necessary for three reasons. It would help to avoid the heterogeneity and hence the disharmony that would result from extending the boundaries and thereby including, like Persia, people of diverse language, religion, history and ethnicity, with almost nothing in common. It was necessary also in order for citizens to acquire the knowledge of the city and of their fellow citizens, from observations, experience and discussion, that would enable them to understand the common good and to distinguish it from their private and personal interests. Finally the small size was essential if citizens were to assemble in order to serve as the sovereign rulers of the city.

4. Fourthly, citizens must be able to assemble and directly decide on the law and decisions of the policy. So deeply held was this view that the Greek found it difficult to conceive of representatives government, must less to accept it as a legitimate alternative to direct democracy.

5. Citizen's participation was not limited, however to the meeting of the assembly. It also included actively partipating in the administration of the city.

6. Finally, the city state must, ideally at least, remain fully autonomous. League, confederacies and alliance might sometimes be necessary for defence or war, but they must not be allowed to preempt the ultimate autonomy of the city states and the sovereignty of the assembly.

Basic Principles of Democracy

1. Liberty:

The main basis of democracy is liberty and equality. The people enjoy maximum liberty and equality because criticism of the people is not only tolerate in this system, but it is also encourage. In Great Britain, the leader of the opposition is paid by the government and he is consulted by the prime minister in national emergency.

For example, when South Rhodesia threatened to declare its freedom unilaterally and when later on it declare its freedom, the British prime minister consulted the leaders of the Conservative party and Liberal party. When Pakistan invaded India during August-September 1965, Prime Minister Lal Bahadur Shastri consulted the leaders of opposite parties before leaving for Tashkent for talk with President Ayub Khan of Pakistan on January 5, 1966.

2. Equality:

Special emphasis is laid on equality in democracy and there is no disparity among the people on the basis of caste, creed, religion and position or status. For example, untouchability has been abolished in India. Beside this, all are equal before law and there is no privileged class in India. It is essential to establish political and economic equality along with social equality. Thus in order to establish political equality, all
disparity on the basis of caste, creed, religion, colour and sex have been removed in India and Adult Franchise has been introduced in order to give opportunity to all the citizens to contest elections to provincial assembly and lok sabha.

3. Fraternity:

Democracy can become successful only in a peaceful atmosphere, otherwise democracy has to face many difficulties. For this purpose Jawaharlal Nehru place an idea of Panch Sheel before the world in 1954. Our government and many other democratic government of the world are making efforts to promote world peace.

4. The people as ultimate source of sovereignty:

In a democracy, people are the ultimate source of sovereignty and the government derives its power from the people. For this purpose, elections takes place in democracies at certain intervals.

5. Fundamental Rights to the People:

In a democracy, people are given fundamental rights because in absence of these rights, the development of an individual is not possible. Fundamental Rights have been granted to the People in their Constitutions in India, Japan, France and Italy.

6. Independence of Judiciary:

In a democracy, it is responsible of the judiciary to protect the fundamental rights of the people. In our country the supreme court and the High Court's protect the constitutional and the fundamental rights of people.

7. The people are considered as an end and State as the means in a democracy:

This is one of the main characteristics of democracy that individual is a mean and the state is an end. It means that the state makes use of the individual for its own interest. In a dictatorship no attention is paid to the freedom of the individual.

Liberal view of Democracy

Liberal democracy, also known as constitutional democracy is a common form of representative democracy. According to the principles of liberal democracy, election should be free and fair and the political process should be competitive. Political pluralism is usually defined as the presence of multiple and distinct political parties.

The Liberal democracies usually have universal suffrage, granting all adults citizens the right to vote regardless of race, gender or property ownership.

Characteristics

Liberalism support the democratic ideas right from the beginning. Its chief features are:

1. It enshrines the supremacy of people;
2. It takes individual as a basic unit of democratic model; assuming that he is rational, ethical, active and self interested;
3. It hated the tyranny of monarchies and aristocracies;
4. It advocated representative government with elected leadership;
5. More than one political party freely competing for political power.

6. Periodic election based on universal adult franchise;
7. Protection of civil liberties;
8. Independence of Judiciary.

Criticism

In spite of being a comprehensive theory of democracy, it has been vehemently criticized on following ground:

1. It ignore the role of organised group, leaders emotions in political affairs.
2. Public opinion as the basis of government is a democratic myth.
3. Democracy become a competition among the elite rather than the masses with the advent of the party system.
4. It based on political equality and economic inequality.
5. According to Marxists, liberal democracies exclusively serve bourgeois interests. It tries to perpetuate the economic division society.

Gandhian view of Democracy

Gandhiji's ideal society was based on democracy without state. It is enlightened anarchy in which social life is based not on external, that is moral restrain. In such a society there is no relationship of command and obedience, superior or inferior. Everybody rules over himself and regulates his own action in the interest of the society because he is a social animal. Gandhiji didn't make any direct suggestions as to the nature of the state. He was a philosophical anarchist and he rejected the state outright and in any of its form. He regarded the state as an instrument on coercion and compulsions which goes on against the free moral development of the individual. The state represents violence in an concentrated and organized form. Since state cannot be completely done away with, it therefore should continue to perform only negative function. So, in fact Gandhiji wanted a non-violence state.

Gandhiji concept of state and democracy is based on truth and non-violence, trusteeship and decentralization. He believed that in a stateless society, there will be proper adjustments between law freedom and social restraint on the basis of dharma. He felt that dislocation came only because state wanted to use violent means which were not acceptable for the people and that this dislocation could be properly adjusted by the means of dharma.

Marxist concept of Democracy

The Marxists do not believe in democracy and talk term of democratic state rather than democratic government. They imply by a democratic state a socialist state in which there is no exploitation and conditions for free development of all exist. They hold that democratic ideals like justice, freedom, equality, etc. cannot be attained so long as the economic exploitation exist in society. Thus the Marxist offered a new meaning and interpretation of democracy. The exposition of the Marxist concept of democracy was given by Lenin in his book "The state and the Revolution". He says "Democracy means equality". The great significance of the proletariat struggle for equality and of equality as a slogan will be clear if we correctly interprets it as meaning the abolition of classes.

Main tenets of Marxist theory of Democracy:

1. The Marxist democracy is based on a system of value and is intimately linked with the abolition of classes.
2. The ultimate objective of Marxist democracy is establishment of a communist society or a stateless society.
3. The Marxian thinker are highly critical of the bourgeoisie democracy and describe it as empty hollow and unreal. This democracy exists only for rich who wield the real power.
4. Though the Marxists are highly critical of bourgeois democracy, they do not admit that it has played an important role in creating political consciousness among the proletariat and encourage them to organise themselves.

5. The Marxian thinker do not provide any details about the stateless or communist society which shall ultimately emerge, although they all hold that it shall be an ideal society in this society there shall be no exploitation and the democratic ideals of freedom, liberty, equality and fraternity shall exist in reality.

6. Marx and Engels never lost their faith in democratic system, but they desire to replace the existing pattern of democracy.

7. The Marxist theory of Democracy appreciate the liberal democracy system for terminating the era of feudalism and instead introducing the system of parliamentary democracy.

Evaluation of Marxist view of Democracy:

Marxian concept of socialist democracy or dictatorship of proletariat has been severely criticised by scholars:

1. It is contended that this type of democracy completely ignored the traditional ideals and value of democracy and lead to the dictatorship of party or the state.
2. This type of dictatorship is dangerous and inimical to the liberty of the people than the dictatorship of individual in so far. It is difficult to replace it.
3. In the Marxists concept of democracy, people are associated with the administration of country without any discrimination of caste, creed, sex, etc. but this exists only in theory.
4. In reality, all the important decisions are taken by party bosses and the common people are merely expected to toe the line indicated by their leaders.
5. The people do not enjoy any right to change their rulers.
6. In absence of any organised opposition, the election becomes a farce and people's participation in the election losses all significance.

Direct Democracy

In simple terms, direct democracy is where political power is exercise by the citizens without representing acting of their behalf. In a direct democracy major decisions on public policy are made directly by the mass of adult citizens.

Direct democracy is also terms as "pure democracy". It can be defined as:

1. A system in which people as a political community come together in a forum to make policy decisions themselves with no intervening institutions or official.
2. A political system in which the citizens vote directly in matter of public concern and every citizen participates in the decisions-making.

As the people participate directly in the administration, direct democracy is best suited for small countries. Swizerland is the one of example of direct democracy where this form of direct democracy puts the steering wheel of government in the hands of the people.

Disadvantages of Direct Democracy:

1. It is votes would require understanding and expertise: In direct democracy, some issues would be black and white and more often than not would involve a complicate set of benefits and drawback that should be examined carefully before votes go out. Citizens then elected the right candidate to answers challenging and complex questions.

2. It could create un-involve and un-educated people: Because direct democracy promote public involvement, people need to get rid all activities and seminars the government would be facilitating.

3. It creates create room for multipopulation and corruption: With direct democracy out in place, every individual can vote directly creating room for multipopulation and corruption like what can be seen in indirect democracy.

4. It poses difficulties in decisions-making: Since this type of system provides greater public involvement, difficulties in decisions-making can be always observed, which is evident government uses decisions that comes from the last equipped citizens, who do not even know what the issues are all about.

5. It instilled the fear of instability:
In the past there have been many situations when the consensus, popular vote was not the right one, which made civil rights immediately coming to mind.

6. It can show down a country's progress:
Unlike in indirect democracy, progress in indirect democracy can be made easily and quickly.

Device of direct democracy

Modern device of direct democracy are as follows:

1. Referendum:
Literary, the term "referendum" means "refer to." It is a device whereby the public opinion or verdicate can be ascertained by a direct reference to the people.

According to Prof. Monobloc, "Referendum is a devices whereby the electoral may veto an act which have a legislative body has already pass."

2. Initiative:
Initiative is the second modern device of direct democracy. It is a positive device by which people have the right to initiative measures for legislation. Under it a fixed portion can submit either a bill or a demand for law-making.
The legislature has to then compulsory upon the measures give its decision. In each case, the bill is submitted to a referendum for a final decision by the people. If the majority of the people approved the bill it becomes a law. If the majority of the people disapproved it, the bill stands rejected.

3. Recall:
Recall is the third popular device of Direct Democracy. It means the power of recall their representatives/legislators who may not be acting according to dictates of public opinion or who may be misusing their authority as the representative of the people. Where prevails, the voters possess the right to call back any elected officers or representative who fails to carry out his duties faithfully.

4. Plebiscite:
The terms 'plebiscite' is of France origin. It means "an appeal to the suffrage of the people." Latin word 'Plebiscitum' which means decree (scitum) of the people (plebis) also constitute a source of the terms plebiscitum. Plebiscite, as such, means the device for knowing public opinion on any issues or problems or policy. It means to know the wish of the people over any particular issue or decision. The verdict is then used by the government as the basis for policy formulation on that issue. According to Leacock "It is used for any kind of popular vote on an issue".

Advantages of Direct Democracy

1. It promotes transparency

The progress and improvement of society can lie in the hands of its people, which means that direct democracy gives people a greater responsibility to deal with fair and honest laws to be implemented.

2. It provides direct responsibility

Since every person has to speak out their needs and worries in direct democracy, government officials and politician would take much care and concern to the people being held accountable for every decision made by the people.

3. It promotes a well – cooperative community

As people have the power to speak for their opinions that the government needs to articulate, a sense of harmonious participation is promoted, which also leads to civic involvement and a meaningful society, where well informed decisions are made not only by the government, but by the public as well.

Indirect Democracy

The prevailing system of democracy is indirect or representative democracy. Here, will of the people is formulated and expresses by their representatives, whom they have delegates the power of discussion and decisions-making representatives are periodically elected by the people for a specific period. J.S. Mill define democracy as one in which "the whole people or the numerous portion of them, exercise the growing power through deputies periodically elected by themselves."

Merits of Democracy

Equality of all

The model of democracy is based on the principles of 'equality of all.' It automatically means 'equal opportunity to all' and 'equal protection of law to all.' Here no discrimination on the ground of caste, creed, colour, religion, etc. are allowed.

Freedom

Under democracy, every citizen is given freedom of speech and expression, free movement anywhere in the country, freedom of religion, freedom of trade/occupation, etc.

Stability

Since democracy, means majority rule, it offers stability. The government enjoys support of maximum number of people.

Responsive government

Under democracy, government is not only responsible to people, it is also responsive to people's needs and public opinion.

Interests of all

Today all over the democratic world, 'welfare state' is an established concept. It means government will be looking after welfare of all people.

World peace

In democracy, the principle of peaceful co-existence is quite important. A democratic set-up will strive for world peace.

Demerits/Disadvantages

Rule of small number

In democracy, smart, manipulative leaders can appeal to people on emotional ground to get votes. Even in a political party, the real power is concentrated in the hands of few. Hence it can be dangerous.

Ignorant ruler

All over the world, whether developed or developing, ordinary citizens are not knowledgeable. They elect somebody from among them who is equally ignorant. Hence democracy becomes a system run by ignorants.

Lack of efficiency

Since democracy means discussion, deliberation the time taken for decisions making is long. This results is inefficientcy.

Corruption

The experience of all democratic societies is educative. One finds corruption at all levels of the administration. Today consisting election have become quite expensive. For this, all corrupt way are used to generate money.

Conditions necessary for the success of Democracy

Educated citizens

A citizen should be knowledgeable about his right and duties. They should be able to protect their rights. Not only this, they should be able to hold government accountable.

Free, Fearless media

Today media is regarded as the fourth pillar of democracy. Media covers newspaper, periodicals radio, TV channel and internet. Media informs people. It air their problems. It criticizes government about its programmes and policies.

Political parties

A good democracy must have well developed party system. If one party is in power, then there should be equally powerful and competent opposition party to oppose the government.

Local self–government

Today it is accepted that local self-government bodies are ideal training ground for the future leaders of democracy. Hence a democratic country must have a good system of local self-government.

Leadership
A democratic system needs a set of good leaders across the political spectrum. Such leader inspire people and make people knowledgeable. They are wise, sensitive and well-read.

Economic security
Since in a democracy, welfare state is a accepted form, it offers economic security of maximum number of people. It creates employment and educational opportunities. It creates a sound public health system.

These are some important conditions of successful democracy.

Challenge to Democracy

Though democracy is like by many societies, it face some serious challenge. These challenge should be studied properly so that one can meet these challenge:

i. Communalism and religious fundamentalism:
This challenge is faced by many democracies. However, in India we also faced communalism which results into communal riot.

ii. Terrorism and militarism:
After 9/11, USA declared that terrorism is the global enemy. India has been facing this problem for many years in Jammu & Kashmir and some North-East state. In other countries like Bangladesh, the danger of military take-over is always present. Today many countries of Asia and Africa are under military rule.

iii. Casteism:
This is a peculiar Indian problem. We have caste-based politics, caste based voting pattern and caste based wars. In the state like Bihar there are inter-caste wars. In many states of Indian union, we find domination caste controlling maximum centre of power.

iv. Criminalization
Increasing criminalization of politics is the real threat to democracy. Here law breakers become law makers. As a result we often witness breakdown of law and order.

v. Corruption:
Whether developed or developing country, corruption is notice at all levels. Political leaders used political power to collect illegal wealth. They use police dept to grant undue favour.

vi. Poverty & illiteracy:
These are unique to Asia and Africa. Here even today many people are illiterate and are quite poor. For the person, what matters is satisfaction of his basic needs-food, shelter and clothes. He is not much worried about democracy.

Similarly an illustrate person can not understand the basic of democratic government.

Advantages of Democracy

1. Responsible and accountable government

The democratic form of government run by elected representatives of the people of the country. It is the people of democratic country who rules the country through their representatives.

2. Equality and fraternity

Democracy preaches the equality and fraternity of men. The idea of equality of man was strengthened by the idea of nationalism.

3. Sense of responsibility among the common people

The achievement of democracy are many. It has infused into the common people a sense of responsibility and power.

4. Self-government

Democracy has gradually become universal because it is inevitable. Man is born with an innate tendency to be free and he can not help feeling that he should govern himself.

5. Development and prosperity for all

Democracy ensure development and prosperity for all. Democracy being the greatest good for large number of people.

6. Popular sovereignty

The supreme power vest the hand common people of the country. If the elected representatives act irresponsibly, then they can dropped in the next election.

7. Sense of cooperation and fraternal feeling

Every citizen, men or women, rich or poor is considered equal in the eyes of law. The feeling of unity, oneness and cooperation is based on the basis of democracy.

Disadvantages

Democracy is the best form of government so far found, but democracy is not without its defect and its critics. In ancient times when states were small, men would gather in a particular place and decide everything by vote. Here democracy was direct.

1. Indirect or representative democracy

As the size of state is becoming larger and larger, we have to content ourselves with indirect or representative democracy. We vote for our representative and it is they who carry on the government and the common man relapse into political indolence.

2. Lack of educated and experienced voters

A large number of un-educated voters participate in the election process. As they have very little to do in matters of government except recording their vote, they have no political experience a become victims of powerful people who deceive them with the large promise and use them for their own private ends.

3. Equal voting rights to both wise, average and innocent person

The common people have no political experience. They do not have the political wisdom. A wise, average and an innocent person have equal voting rights. Ignorant people may or may not vote for the right candidate.

4. Freedom to all shades of opinions

Another charge against democracy is that as it gives freedom of expression to all the shades of opinion. It easily leads to the formation of parties and party government only means talk and talk and talk, democratic parliaments being more or less dignified debating society.

5. Delay in decisions making process

The power is not centralized which delays the decisions-making process. A number of formalities are to be observed in decision making and adopting process. At times, it becomes difficult to take measures in the best interest of the country. This acts as an hindrance for economic growth and development.

CHAPTER IX

Procedural Democracy and it's critique

1) 'Procedure' and 'Procedural From of Democracy':

Procedure can be defined as a proccess or system for accomplishing something. It signifies a particular course of action. Procedure and Process are not synonymous. A process may be defined as a series of actions to achieve an end or aim. But procedure is to be considered as a series of actions which are conducted in a certain manner or in an established way of doing or achieving something. Procedure implies action, course, operation or modus operand. It emphasizes a routine or a strategy or a game plan. The result or the end or aims is of course important, but much more important is the way of transation. Simply speaking, it basically focuses on the method of doing something. It is like a set of guidelines that one would follow in order to complete a task. Most often a procedure lists some details that are to be followed to achieve an end. The formation of these details is a highly scientific task which is carried on by experts who provide step by step explanation of conducting a procedure which is the centre of attention. How to explain about the procedure which best results into a democracy? Of course, it is through a detailed description of which has to be followed in order to achieve the objective by law. That, if this procedure is followed, the automatically result would be a perfect democracy. Through law, through the constitution, details are prescribed as to how to bring about and maintain a democracy.

2) Emergence or origion of procedural democracy:

The emergence of a procedural definition of democracy can be traced back to the writing of Joseph Schumpeter. In his book "Capitalism, socialism and democracy (1942)", Schumpeter replaced the classical definitions of democracy which depicted it as 'the rule of the people' or 'rule of the common good'. Instead he provide a notion of the democratic method. For Schumpeter the democratic method is a type of institional arrangement by way of which political decisions can be arrived. For Schumpeter, through this method individuals acquire the power to decide and make policies.

Procedural democracy clearly encapsulates the mind malist conception of democracy. It only recognizes a minimum level of freedom of assembly, speech, organization and press. It dose not incorporate them as the determiner or actual measures of democracy.

Another major book "Democracy and Development" written by Adam Przeworski states that "democracy is a regime in which those who govern are selected through contested elections." This book provides a classification of democracies and distatorships covering all countries in the world between the years 1946 to 1999.

Procedural theory seems to give credence to the anti-democratis logic of the elitist theory of democracy. The elitist theory eulogizes the argument in favour of limited political participation and limited franchise. The understanding of democracy posits that for a society to be considered democratic, it should be governed by a particular set of procedures, which derive from some specific ingredient, which are:

1) Free and fair elections are the hallmark of democracy: Procedural democracy is mainly characterised by citizens choosing to elect their representative in free elections. It assumes that a fair elector procedure is the core of democracy. Therefore all procedures of election, as established by law, should be duly complied with. There should also be enough provision for governmental, as well as independent bodies or organizations, to ensure compliance of due procedure of elections.

2) Procedural democracy focuses on the competition of political parties in an electoral system: Ensurity of free and fair competition among parties is necessary for the functioning of democracy. Law and constitution should clearly prescribe rules and guidelines for political parties to follow the due procedure of elections. It is mainly through political parties that the representative government of the people is established. Political parties control the legislature and bring out policies and new laws and run the government. Therefore free and fair competition among parties should be ensured by providing clear procedural guidelines to political parties by a way of law.

3) Another basic ingredient of procedural democracy is universal suffrage, which indicates the right to vote by all adult citizens of a country. In other words, universal suffrage or universal adult franchise implies the right of all adult citizens to vote without any discrimination of caste, creed, gender, colour, race, educational qualification and economic status. Procedural or otherwise, democracy hinges upon the idea of one person/one vote political equality. It indicates that the right to participate in the voting process should be available to all the adult citizens of a country.

4) Another important ingredient of the procedural aspect of democracy is neutrality or procedural fairness: Principle of neutrality procedural democracy implies that the state and government should provide a neutral framework of rights and the citizens should be free to choose their own values and end. The latent idea is that the government should not enforce, through its policies and law, any particular conception of good life. That means governance should be devoid of any hard ideological inclination, other than of benefit to citizens. Political ideologies should not particularly guide any democracy. Democracy in itself the ideology. Procedural fairness requires that the government should be totally secular. It should not be partial and respect the belief or practices of all groups in a society. It should be totally detached or non partisan so far as the conceptions of good life are concerned. The procedural finiteness would itself lead to the ultimate democratic goodness of life citizens.

CHAPTER X

Deliberative Democracy

Deliberative democracy or discursive democracy is a form of democracy in which deliberation is central to decision-making. It adopts elements of both consensus decision-making and majority rule. Deliberative democracy differs from traditional democratic theory in that authentic deliberation, not mere voting, is the primary source of legitimacy for the law. Deliberative democracy is closely related to consultative democracy, in which public consultation with citizens is central to democratic processes.

While deliberative democracy is generally seen as some form of an amalgam of representative democracy and direct democracy, the actual relationship is usually open to dispute. Some practitioners and theorists use the term to encompass representative bodies whose members authentically and practically deliberate on legislation without unequal distributions of power, while others use the term exclusively to refer to decision-making directly by lay citizens, as in direct democracy.

The term "deliberative democracy" was originally coined by Joseph M. Bessette in his 1980 work Deliberative Democracy: The Majority Principle in Republican Government.

Deliberative democracy holds that, for a democratic decision to be legitimate, it must be preceded by authentic deliberation, not merely the aggregation of preferences that occurs in voting. Authentic deliberation is deliberation among decision-makers that is free from distortions of unequal political power, such as power a decision-maker obtained through economic wealth or the support of interest groups. If the decision-makers cannot reach consensus after authentically deliberating on a proposal, then they vote on the proposal using a form of majority rule.

The roots of deliberative democracy can be traced back to Aristotle and his notion of politics; however, the German philosopher Jürgen Habermas‘ work on communicative rationality and the public sphere is often identified as a major work in this area.

Deliberative democracy can be practiced by decision-makers in both representative democracies and direct democracies. In elitist deliberative democracy, principles of deliberative democracy apply to elite societal decision-making bodies, such as legislatures and courts; in populist deliberative democracy, principles of deliberative democracy apply to groups of lay citizens who are empowered to make decisions. One purpose of populist deliberative democracy can be to use deliberation among a group of lay citizens to distill a more authentic public opinion about societal issues but not directly create binding law; devices such as the deliberative opinion poll have been designed to achieve this goal. Another purpose of populist deliberative democracy can be to serve as a form of direct democracy, where deliberation among a group of lay citizens forms a "public will" and directly creates binding law. If political decisions are made by deliberation but not by the people themselves or their elected representatives, then there is no democratic element; this deliberative process is called elite deliberation. According to Fishkin, this process attempts to indirectly filter the mass public opinion because representatives are better equipped with the knowledge of the common good than ordinary citizens.

Characteristics

Fishkin's model of deliberation

James Fishkin, who has designed practical implementations of deliberative democracy for over 15 years in various countries, describes five characteristics essential for legitimate deliberation:

Information: The extent to which participants are given access to reasonably accurate information that they believe to be relevant to the issue.

Substantive balance: The extent to which arguments offered by one side or from one perspective are answered by considerations offered by those who hold other perspectives.

Diversity: The extent to which the major position in the public are represented by participants in the discussion.

Conscientiousness: The extent to which participants sincerely weigh the merits of the arguments.

Equal consideration: The extent to which arguments offered by all participants are considered on the merits regardless of which participants offer them.

In Fishkin's definition of deliberative democracy, lay citizens must participate in the decision-making process, thus making it a subtype of direct democracy.

James Fishkin and Robert Luskin suggest that deliberative discussion should be:

Informed (and thus informative). Arguments should be supported by appropriate and reasonably accurate factual claims.

Balanced. Arguments should be met by contrary arguments.

Conscientious. The participants should be willing to talk and listen, with civility and respect.

Substantive. Arguments should be considered sincerely on their merits, not on how they are made or by who is making them.

Comprehensive. All points of view held by significant portions of the population should receive attention.

Cohen's outline

Joshua Cohen, a student of John Rawls, outlined conditions that he thinks constitute the root principles of the theory of deliberative democracy, in the article "Deliberation and Democratic Legitimacy" in the 1989 book The Good Polity. He outlines five main features of deliberative democracy, which include:

An ongoing independent association with expected continuation.

The citizens in the democracy structure their institutions such that deliberation is the deciding factor in the creation of the institutions and the institutions allow deliberation to continue.

A commitment to the respect of a pluralism of values and aims within the polity.

The citizens consider deliberative procedure as the source of legitimacy and prefer the causal history of legitimation for each law to be transparent and easily traceable to the deliberative process.

Each member recognizes and respects other members' deliberative capacity.

This can be construed as the idea that in the legislative process, we "owe" one another reasons for our proposals.

Cohen presents deliberative democracy as more than a theory of legitimacy and forms a body of substantive rights around it based on achieving "ideal deliberation":

It is free in two ways:

The participants consider themselves bound solely by the results and preconditions of the deliberation. They are free from any authority of prior norms or requirements.

The participants suppose that they can act on the decision made; the deliberative process is a sufficient reason to comply with the decision reached.

Parties to deliberation are required to state reasons for their proposals and proposals are accepted or rejected based on the reasons given, as the content of the very deliberation taking place.

Participants are equal in two ways:

Formal: anyone can put forth proposals, criticize and support measures. There is no substantive hierarchy.

Substantive: The participants are not limited or bound by certain distributions of power, resources or pre-existing norms. "The participants do not regard themselves as bound by the existing system of rights, except in so far as that system establishes the framework of free deliberation among equals."

Deliberation aims at a rationally motivated consensus: It aims to find reasons acceptable to all who are committed to such a system of decision-making. When consensus or something near enough is not possible, majoritarian decision making is used.

In Democracy and Liberty, an essay published in 1998, Cohen reiterated many of these points, also emphasizing the concept of "reasonable pluralism" – the acceptance of different, incompatible worldviews and the importance of good faith deliberative efforts to ensure that as far as possible the holders of these views can live together on terms acceptable to all.

Gutmann and Thompson's model

Amy Gutmann and Dennis F. Thompson's definition captures the elements that are found in most conceptions of deliberative democracy. They define it as "a form of government in which free and equal citizens and their representatives justify decisions in a process in which they give one another reasons that are mutually acceptable and generally accessible, with the aim of reaching decisions that are binding on all at present but open to challenge in the future".

They state that deliberative democracy has four requirements, which refer to the kind of reasons that citizens and their representatives are expected to give to one another:

Reciprocal. The reasons should be acceptable to free and equal persons seeking fair terms of cooperation.

Accessible. The reasons must be given in public and the content must be understandable to the relevant audience.

Binding. The reason-giving process leads to a decision or law that is enforced for some period of time. The participants do not deliberate just for the sake of deliberation or for individual enlightenment.

Dynamic or Provisional. The participants must keep open the possibility of changing their minds and continuing a reason-giving dialogue that can challenge previous decisions and laws.

Strengths and weaknesses

A claimed strength of deliberative democratic models is that they are more easily able to incorporate scientific opinion and base policy on outputs of ongoing research, because:

Time is given for all participants to understand and discuss the science

Scientific peer review, adversarial presentation of competing arguments, refereed journals, even betting markets are also deliberative processes.

The technology used to record dissent and document opinions opposed to the majority is also useful to notarize bets, predictions and claims.

Deliberative ideals often include "face-to-face discussion, the implementation of good public policy, decisionmaking competence and critical mass." According to proponents such as James Fearon, another strength of deliberative democratic models is that they tend, more than any other model, to generate ideal conditions of impartiality, rationality and knowledge of the relevant facts. The more these conditions are fulfilled, the greater the likelihood that the decisions reached are morally correct. Deliberative democracy takes on the role of an "epistemic democracy" in this way, as it thus has an epistemic value: it allows participants to deduce what is morally correct. This view has been prominently held by Carlos Nino.

Studies by James Fishkin and others have found that deliberative democracy tends to produce outcomes which are superior to those in other forms of democracy. Deliberative democracy produces less partisanship and more sympathy with opposing views; more respect for evidence-based reasoning rather than opinion; a greater commitment to the decisions taken by those involved; and a greater chance for widely shared consensus to emerge, thus promoting social cohesion between people from different backgrounds. Fishkin cites extensive empirical support for the increase in public spiritedness that is often caused by participation in deliberation and says theoretical support can be traced back to foundational democratic thinkers such as John Stuart Mill and Alexis de Tocqueville. Former diplomat Carne Ross writes that in 2011 that the debates arising from deliberative democracy are also much more civil, collaborative and evidence-based than the debates in traditional town hall meetings or in internet forums. For Ross, the key reason for this is that in deliberative democracy citizens are empowered by knowledge that their debates will have a measurable impact on society.

Efforts to promote public participation have been widely critiqued. There is particular concern regarding the potential capture of the public into the sphere of influence of governance stakeholders, leaving communities frustrated by public participation initiatives, marginalized and ignored.

A claimed failure of most theories of deliberative democracy is that they do not address the problems of voting. James Fishkin's 1991 work, "Democracy and Deliberation", introduced a way to apply the theory of deliberative democracy to real-world decision making, by way of what he calls the deliberative opinion poll. In the deliberative opinion poll, a statistically representative sample of the nation or a community is gathered to discuss an issue in conditions that further deliberation. The group is then polled and the results of the poll and the actual deliberation can be used both as a recommending force and in certain circumstances, to replace a vote. Dozens of deliberative opinion polls have been conducted across the United States since his book was published.

The political philosopher Charles Blattberg has criticized deliberative democracy on four grounds: (i) the rules for deliberation that deliberative theorists affirm interfere with, rather than facilitate, good practical reasoning; (ii) deliberative democracy is ideologically biased in favor of liberalism as well as republican over parliamentary democratic systems; (iii) deliberative democrats assert a too-sharp division between just and rational deliberation on the one hand and self-interested and coercive bargaining or negotiation on the other; and (iv) deliberative democrats encourage an adversarial relationship between state and society, one that undermines solidarity between citizens.

A criticism of deliberation is that potentially it allows those most skilled in rhetoric to sway the decision in their favour. This criticism has been made since deliberative democracy first arose in Ancient Athens.

The agonistic perspective on deliberative democracy

Deliberative theories of democracy have often been contrasted with agonistic models of democracy. Theorists of agonism such as Chantal Mouffe, Ernesto Laclau and William E. Connolly reject the possibility of reaching consensus through deliberation. In particular, Mouffe questions the empirical attainability of consensus in post-Cold War democracies.

Firstly, the consensus on the superiority of neoliberalism – which was believed to have been forged with the collapse of the USSR and the delegitimisation of communism as an ideological antidote to capitalism – is no longer as strong as it was in the wake of the dissolution of the USSR. Realising the failures of neoliberalism, such as massive economic inequality and the exploitations arising from capitalist practices, there is greater division on the issue of how best to organise societies globally today. Secondly, with the rise of identity politics in the West, people are less reliant on traditional parties for political representation, often believing that they have lost their ability to take their interests into account.

Together, agonistic theorists question whether consensus as a democratic approach is even appropriate because of its inability to embrace difference. To them, difference is an inerradicable condition of human existence; to pursue consensus is to assimilate identities into a universal category of neoliberal subjectivity, which can lead to various forms of coercion and exclusion. Accordingly, the lack of closure in politics, the "ongoing confrontation," is to be seen not as a sign of failure but a testament to the vibrancy of democracies.

Some academics do not think a clear-cut opposition between deliberative and agonistic theories can be identified. For example, drawing on the work of Hannah Arendt, Shmuel Lederman laments the fact that "deliberation and agonism have become almost two different schools of thought" that are discussed as "mutually exclusive conceptions of politics". Similarly, Giuseppe Ballacci argue that agonism and deliberation are not only compatible but mutually dependent: "a properly understood agonism requires the use of deliberative skills but also that even a strongly deliberative politics could not be completely exempt from some of the consequences of agonism".

History

Consensus-based decision making similar to deliberative democracy is characteristic of the hunter-gatherer band societies thought to predominate in pre-historical times. As some of these societies became more complex with developments like division of labour, community-based decision making was displaced by various forms of authoritarian rule. The first example of democracy arose in Greece as Athenian democracy during the sixth century BC. Athenian democracy was both deliberative and largely direct: some decisions were made by representatives but most were made by "the people" directly. Athenian democracy came to an end in 322BC. When democracy was revived as a political system about 2000 years later, decisions were made by representatives rather than directly by the people. In a sense, this revived version was deliberative from its beginnings; for example, in 1774 Edmund Burke made a famous speech where he called Great Britain's parliament a deliberative assembly. Similarly, the Founding Fathers of the United States considered deliberation an essential part of the government they created in the late 18th century.

The deliberative element of democracy was not widely studied by academics until the late 20th century. Although some of the seminal work was done in the 1970s and 80s, it was only in 1990 that deliberative democracy began to attract substantial attention from political scientists. According to Professor John Dryzek, early work on deliberative democracy was part of efforts to develop a theory of democratic legitimacy. Theorists such as Carne Ross advocate deliberative democracy as a complete alternative to representative democracy. The more common view, held by contributors such as James Fishkin, is that direct deliberative democracy can be complementary to traditional representative democracy. Since 1994, hundreds of implementations of direct deliberative democracy have taken place throughout the world. For example, lay citizens have used deliberative democracy to determine local budget allocations in various cities and to undertake major public projects, such as the rebuilding of New Orleans after Hurricane Katrina.

Association with political movements

Call for the establishment of deliberative democracy on the Rally to Restore Sanity and/or Fear

Deliberative democracy recognizes a conflict of interest between the citizen participating, those affected or victimized by the process being undertaken and the group-entity that organizes the decision. Thus it usually involves an extensive outreach effort to include marginalized, isolated, ignored groups in decisions and to extensively document dissent, grounds for dissent and future predictions of consequences of actions. It focuses as much on the process as the results. In this form it is a complete theory of civics.

On the other hand, many practitioners of deliberative democracy attempt to be as neutral and open-ended as possible, inviting (or even randomly selecting) people who represent a wide range of views and providing them with balanced materials to guide their discussions. Examples include National Issues Forums, Choices for the 21st Century, study circles, deliberative opinion polls, the Citizens' Initiative Review and the 21st-century town meetings convened by America Speaks, among others. In these cases, deliberative democracy is not connected to left-wing politics but is intended to create a conversation among people of different philosophies and beliefs.

In Canada, there have been two prominent applications of deliberative democratic models. In 2004, the British Columbia Citizens' Assembly on Electoral Reform convened a policy jury to consider alternatives to the first-past-the-post electoral systems. In 2007, the Ontario Citizens' Assembly on Electoral Reform convened to consider alternative electoral systems in that province. Similarly, three of Ontario's Local Health Integration Networks (LHIN) have referred their budget priorities to a policy jury for advice and refinement.

The Green Party of the United States refers to its particular proposals for grassroots democracy and electoral reform by this name. Although not always the case, participation in deliberation has often been found to shift participants opinions in favour of Green positions and can even cause a favourable change of voting intention. For example, with Europolis 2009, at the time one of the largest deliberative assemblies ever held, which set out to assess the public's view on a wide range of issues and included representatives from all 27 EU member nations, the share of citizens intending to vote for the Greens increased from 8% to 18%.

Academic contributors

According to Professor Stephen Tierney, perhaps the earliest notable example of academic interest in the deliberative aspects of democracy occurred in John Rawls 1971 work A Theory of Justice.

Joseph M. Bessette coined the term "deliberative democracy" in his 1980 work "Deliberative Democracy: The Majority Principle in Republican Government" and went on to elaborate and defend the notion in "The Mild Voice of Reason" (1994). Others contributing to the notion of deliberative democracy include Carlos Nino, Jon Elster, Roberto Gargarella, John Gastil, Jürgen Habermas, David Held, Joshua Cohen, John Rawls, Amy Gutmann, Noëlle McAfee, John Dryzek, Rense Bos, James S. Fishkin, Jane Mansbridge, Jose Luis Marti, Dennis Thompson, Benny Hjern, Hal Koch, Seyla Benhabib, Ethan Leib, Charles Sabel, Jeffrey K. Tulis, David Estlund, Mariah Zeisberg, Jeffrey L. McNairn, Iris Marion Young and Robert B. Talisse.

Although political theorists took the lead in the study of deliberative democracy, political scientists have in recent years begun to investigate its processes. One of the main challenges currently is to discover more about the actual conditions under which the ideals of deliberative democracy are more or less likely to be realized.

Most recently, scholarship has focused on the emergence of a 'systemic approach' to the study of deliberation. This suggests that the deliberative capacity of a democratic system needs to be understood through the interconnection of the variety of sites of deliberation which exist, rather than any single setting. Some studies have conducted experiments to examine how deliberative democracy addresses the problems of sustainability and underrepresentation of future generations.

CHAPTER XI

Participation and Representation

Democracy involves popular control over decision making and equality between citizens in the exercise of that control. Popular control over decision making is achieved through inclusive political participation and representation in democratic institutions and processes in which each citizen has an equal right and opportunity to engage in and contribute to decision making. Without citizen participation , and the rights, freedoms and means to participate, the principle of popular control over government cannot begin to be realized. Without representation, public institutions that are socially representative of citizens cannot be developed.

Political participation and representation go beyond the act of voting in elections; they also embody the freedom of citizens to empress their opinions and to mobilize to influence policy. Together, they ensure that democracy and democratic institutions are a genuine reflection of the will of the citizens.

Participation and representation are two fundamental elements and principles of democracy. They affirm that a democracy is dependent on its citizens and that this ownership is expressed through meaningful participation by and representation of all citizens in democratic institutions and processes.

Underpinning all this is the idea that every citizen, regardless of class, age, gender, sexual orientation, ability, group, culture and ethnic or religious background, should have an equal right and opportunity to engage with and contribute to the functioning of these institutions and processes. The goal of any undertaking in this field is clear: to assist political institutions to become more responsive, responsible and representative. Political institutions and processes include political parties, parliaments and governments and their interactions with society. Responsiveness means that governments are able to react to the demands and needs of society at large , and that they are ready to openly and transparently interact with a variety of actors , including civil society. Responsibility means that governments can be held accountable by citizen. Representativeness means that governments work on institutionalizing political life and public political participation through legitimate institutions.

Supporting participation and representation today, however, remains a challenge. Perhaps the greatest of the challenges faced by democracies globally is how to connect people's needs and aspirations with accountable and representative political institutions. Some citizens, in all countries irrespective of their stage of democratic development, have come to mistrust their institutions. Often, citizens are not interested in participating in political processes in their traditional form, including in elections, in the belief that it makes no difference who is in power, that political institutions will do whatever they want and that the voice of citizen does not have a sufficient level of influence.

Despite their fundamental importance to democracy, promoting and ensuring inclusive political participation and representation are still challenges for today. Democracies are not always able to provide equal opportunities for inclusive political participation and representation. Many citizens, in both established and newer democracies, are losing trust in existing political institutions and processes, which are seen as dominated by a select number of group of elites. Unequal opportunities for participation and representation between man and women still exist worldwide. Minorities are still unable to participate or represent their interests in democratic institutions and processes.

Inequality of opportunity persists worldwide. Not all citizens in society are represented in policy discussion and many feel marginalized. Women, who constitute over 50 per cent of the world's population, continue to be underrepresented as voters, political leaders and elected officials.

Democracy cannot truly deliver for all of its citizens if half the population remains excluded from the political arena. Women's equal representation is a matter of justice and democracy. Democracy is not only about the right to vote – it is also about the right to be elected.

In some cases, access to political institutions is not available or even feasible because the frameworks or modalities for inclusive citizen involvement and engagement are not being implemented or are simply not in place. It is in this context that promoting inclusive political participation and representation remain priorities for all democratic Nation – Stages, civil societies, international organizations, regional organizations act across the globe.

To summarize the background notes – participation and representation are two fundamental elements and principles of democracy. They affirm that a democracy is dependent on its citizens and that this ownership is expressed through meaningful participation by and representation of all citizens in democratic institutions and processes. Underpinning all this is the idea that every citizen, regardless of class, age, gender, sexual orientation, ability, group, culture and ethnic or religious background, should have an equal right and opportunity to engage with and contribute to the functioning of these institutions and processes. This is the key to an inclusive and truly participatory.

Defining Political Representation:

In politics, representation describes how some individuals stand in for others or a group of others, for a certain time period. Representation usually refers to representative democracies, where elected officials nominally speak for their constituents in the legislature. Generally, only citizens are granted representation in the government in the form of voting rights; however, some democracies have extended this right further. The term ' representation ' comes from the Latin word 'repraesentatio' meaning representation gained its contemporary denotation of political representation with all its implications in the era of the French Revolution of 1789 . The earlier terms, such as mandatum , concilia, colloquia, conventus , curiae , placita etc., did not reflect the meaning of the term 'representation', although it much be admitted that some of them, such as mandate, were closely related to this term. It was then that the concept of the mandate , and specifically representation, took on its public legal character, becoming in a short time the most fundamental constitutional concept both in the constitutional law theory as well as in legislation at a constitutional level, which more or less openly accepted the principles of political representation construing it into a political principle of a State. For fullfiling the principles of representative and participatory democracy viz . Liberty, equality, justice needs political representation – a must have.

British politician Edmund Burke in his 1774 Speech to the Electors at Bristol at the Conclusion of the poll was noted for his articulation of the principles of representation against the nation that elected officials should be delegates how exactly mirror the opinions of the electorate.

Hanna Pitkin in her epochal work "The concept of political representation" (1967) provides, perhaps, one of the most straightforward definitions : to represent is simply to "make present again." On this definition, political representation is the activity of making citizens' voices, opinions and perspectives "present" in public policy making processes. Political representation occurs when political actors speak , advocate, symbolize , and act on the behalf of others in the political arena. In short, political representation is a kind of political assistance.

Types or Typology of political representation:

1) Substantive Representation: Under representative democracy, substantive representation is the tendency of elected legislators to advocate on behalf of certain groups. Conflicting theories and beliefs exist regarding why constituents vote for representative. "Rather than choosing candidates on the basis of an informed view of the incumbents' voting records, voters, it is argued, rely primarily on the policy-free 'symbols' of party identification." Politicians, it would seem, have little to fear from a public that knows little about what laws their representatives support or oppose in the legislature.

2) Descriptive Representation: It is the idea elected representatives in democracies should represent not only the expressed preferences of their constituencies (or the nation as a whole) but also those of their descriptive characteristics that are politically relevant, such as geographical area of birth, occupation, ethnicity or gender. For example, according to this idea, an elected body should resemble a representative

sample of the voters they are meant to represent concerning outward characteristics – a constituency of 50% women and 20% blacks, for example, should have 50% female and 20% black legislators. Sometimes voting systems that obtain proportional representation may achieve descriptive representation as well. However this can be guaranteed only to the extent that voting patterns reflect descriptive characteristics of the voters.

3) Dyadic Representation: It refers to the degree to which and ways by which elected legislators represent the preferences or interests of the specific geographic constituencies from which they are elected. Candidates who run for legislative office in an individual constituency or as a member of a party candidates are especially motivated to provide dyadic representation. As Carey and Shugart observed that they have "incentives to cultivate a personal vote" beyond whatever support their party label will produce. Personal vote seeking might arise from representing the public policy interests of the constituency (by way of either the delegate, responsible party or trustee models noted above), providing it "pork barrel" goods, offering service to individual constituents as by helping them acquire government services and symbolic action.

Example: The most abundant scientific scholarship on dyadic representation has been for the U.S. Congress (especially and more particulary for its upper chamber/house i.e. senate in which each of US state are equally represented with 2 members each from 50 states [i .e. 50×2=100 US Senators] who are directly or popularly elected an for policy representation of constituencies by the members of the Congress.

4) Collective Representation: The concept of collective representation can be found in various normative theory and scientific works, but Weissberg offered the first systematic characterization of it the scientific literature and for the U.S. Congress, defining such representation as "Whether Congress as an institution represents the American people, not whether each member of Congress represented his or her particular district." Hurley (1982) elaborated and qualified weissberg's explication of how such representation should be assessed and how it relates to dyadic representation. Stimson, MacKuen and Erikson (1995) offer the most advanced theoretical exposition of such representation for the U.S. Congress. And the latter work was extended in Erikson, MacKuen and Stimson (2002).

In most parliamentary political systems with strong (or ideologically unified) political parties and where the election system is dominated by parties instead of individual candidates, the primary basis for representation is also a collective, party based one. The foundational work on assessing such representation is that of Huber and Powell (1994) and Powell (2000).

Theorizing political representation: Pitkin's four theories or views of representation

Hanna Fenichel Pitkin established four theories or views of representation in her major work "The Concept of Representation" (1967). At present, this work has been considered the most definitive and comprehensive theorization (thought not perfect or final) of the concept of political representation.

Pitkin has in many set the terms of contemporary discussions about representation by providing this schematic overview of the concept of political representation.

1) Formalistic Representation: The institutional arrangements that preccede and initiate representation. Formal representation has two dimensions: Authorization and Accountability.

a) Authorization - The means by which a representative obtains his or her standing, status, position or office. No standards for assessing how well a representative behaves. One can merely assess whatever a representative legitimately holds his or her position.

b) Accountability – The ability of constituents to punish their representative for failing to act in accordance with their wishes (for example, voting and elected official out of office) or the responsiveness of the representative to the constituents.

2) Symbolic Representation: The ways that a representative "stands for" the represented – that is the meaning that a representative has for those being represented. Representatives are assessed by the degree of acceptance that the representative has among the represented.

3) Descriptive Representation: The extent to which a representative resembles those being represented. Assess the representative by the accuracy of the resemblance between the representative and the represented.

4) Substantive Representation: The activity of representatives – that is, the actions taken on behalf of in the interest of, as an agent of, and as a substitute for the represented. Assess a representative by the extent to which policy outcomes advanced by a representative serve "the best interests" of their constituents.

Critical Evaluation of Pitkin's Theories/Views of Political Representation:

One cannot overestimate the extent to which Pitkin has shaped contemporary understanding of political representation, especially among political scientists. For example, her claim that descriptive representation opposes accountability is often the starting point for contemporary discussions about whether marginalized group need representatives from their group.

Similarly, Pitkin's conclusions about the paradoxical nature of political representation support the tendency among contemporary theorists and political scientists to focus on formal procedures of authorization and accountability (formalistic representation). In particular, there has been a lot of theoretical attention paid to the proper design of representative institutions. This focus is certainly understandable, since one way to resolve the disputes about what representatives should be doing is to "let the people decide." In other words, establishing fair procedure for reconciling conflicts provides democratic citizens one way to settle conflicts about the proper behavior of representatives. In this way, theoretical discussions of political representation tend to depict political representation as primarily a principal- agent relationship. The emphasis on elections also explains why discussions about the concept of political representation frequently collapse in to discussions of democracy. Political representation is not just for merely about holding periodic election but is understood as a way of

1) establishing the legitimacy of democratic institutions and 2) creating institutional incentives for governments to be responsive to citizens.

David Plotke has noted that this emphasis on mechanism of authorization and accountability was especially useful in the context of the cold war. For this understanding of political representation (specifically, its demarcation from participatory democracy) was useful for distinguishing western democracies from communist countries. Those political systems that held competitive elections were considered to be democratic. Plotke questions whether such a distinction continues to be useful. Plotke recommends that we broaden the scope of our understanding of political representation to encompass interest representation and thereby return to debating what is the proper activity of representatives.

Plotke's insight into why traditional understandings of political representation resonated prior to the end of the cold war suggests that modern understanding of political representation are to some extent contingent on political realities. For this reason, those who attempt to define political representation should recognize how challenging political realities can affect contemporary understandings of political representation. Again, following Pitkin, ideas about political representation appear contingent on existing political practices of representation. Our understanding of representation are inextricably shaped by the manner in which people are currently being represented.

Critic of political representation as a concept in politics and political science:

In his book "political parties", written in 1911, Robert Michels argues that most representative systems deteriorate towards an oligarchy or particracy. This is known as the "iron law of oligarchy".

Representative democracies which are stable have been analysed by German political thinker Adolf Gasser and compared to the unstable representative democracies in his book written in German or Deutsch language "Gemeindefreiheit als Rettung Europas" which was published in 1943. Adolf Gesser stated that following requirements for a representative democracy in order to remain stable, unaffected by the iron law of oligarchy:

a) Society has to be built up from bottom to top. As a consequence, society is built up by people, who are free and have the power to defend themselves with weapons.
b) These free people join or form local communities. These local communities are independent, which includes financial independence and they are free to determine their own rules.
c) Local communities join together into a higher unit e.g. a Canton.
d) There is no hierarchical bureaucracy.
e) There is competition between these local communities e.g. on services delivered or no taxes.

A drawback to his type of government is that elected officials are not required to fulfill promises made before their election and are able to promote their own self-interests once elected, providing an incohesive system of governmence. Legislators are also under scrutiny as the system of majority - won legislators voting for issues for the large group of people fosters inequality among the marginalized.

Solution: Possible solution to the drawbacks of political representation in the 21st century can be making deliberative democracy more inclusive and representative viz. for example give 33% women representation in India at the panchayat level, making governments more responsive by way of using digital tools like social media (example - www.mygov.in by PM Narendra Modi in India or Janatar Sarkar intiative by CM Sarbananda Sonowal of Assam as a ideal way gov-public interface) turning deleberative democracy into 'digital/internet/e-democracy', functional representation (that is earmarking some constituencies for particular member representing particular function or profession viz. a constituency only for engineers where only engineers will vote and elect an engineer to represent them and their profession etc.).

9 798889 594161

Printed by Libri Plureos GmbH in Hamburg,
Germany